A Catholic Survival Guide for Times of Emergency

A CATHOLIC SURVIVAL GUIDE FOR TIMES OF EMERGENCY

Deacon Nick Donnelly

TAN Books
Gastonia, North Carolina

Cover design by Caroline Green

Cover image: Compass with Christian Cross by Haali / Shutterstock

ISBN: 978-1-5051-1869-8
Kindle ISBN: 978-1-5051-1870-4
EPUB ISBN: 978-1-5051-1871-1

Published in the United States by
TAN Books
PO Box 269
Gastonia, NC 28053
www.TANBooks.com

Printed in the United States of America

Contents

Preface

This short book was written during the lockdown in response to the COVID-19 pandemic, amidst the daily news reports of the rising death toll around the world. It originated in three articles I wrote for the traditional Catholic website *Rorate Caeli*, the first one published in early March 2020 on the Act of Perfect Contrition and Spiritual Communion. As the pandemic emerged, I was concerned for the pastoral and spiritual care of my fellow Catholics in the eventuality that our churches were closed and we were deprived of the sacraments and the assistance of our priests, which is in fact what tragically happened to countless Catholics around the world.

I'm very grateful to everyone who helped me get the message out to the faithful about how traditional devotions give access during an emergency to the saving grace and wisdom of Almighty God. With the invaluable assistance of faithful around the world who contacted me via twitter, I was able to provide a step-by-step guide to perfect contrition and spiritual communion translated into six languages. My grateful thanks to *Church Militant* for making these guides available to download to help as many as possible. And thanks to Virgin Most Powerful Radio's *Jesus 911* show for dedicating an entire broadcast to my promotion of perfect contrition and spiritual communion. Also, thanks to *LifeSite News, Gloria TV, Adelante la fe*, and *The Meaning of Catholic*.

Though this book took shape in response to the Wuhan coronavirus pandemic, it has been written to help Catholics draw on the graces and wisdom of the Faith to cope with national, community, or personal emergencies. No matter what life brings, may we always "live in the shelter of the Most High."

> You who live in the shelter of the Most High,
> who abide in the shadow of the Almighty,
> will say to the Lord, "My refuge and my fortress;
> my God, in whom I trust."
> For he will deliver you from the snare of the fowler
> and from the deadly pestilence. (Ps 91:1–3)

Deacon Nick Donnelly BA (Hons) Div, MA
29 April 2020, Feast of St. Catherine of Siena

What to Do When Deprived of Confession or Holy Communion

Recourse to the sacraments is essential to the supernatural lives of Catholics. This is even more true during times of crisis. When facing an emergency, we need the inner peace, strength, and resolve that comes from the forgiveness of our sins; we need the faithful certainty, intimate presence, and guidance of Our Lord that comes from Holy Communion. But more than this, when facing life-threatening emergencies, we need to know that we are in a state of sanctifying grace, and are righteous through the grace of God, in case we die and face our individual judgment.

Living in a stable, democratic country that upholds religious freedom, we have the expectation that we will receive the pastoral assistance of our clergy and the sacraments during times of emergency. However, the COVID-19 pandemic has shown us how fragile our sacramental life really is when an overwhelming national emergency hits our society. Witnessing the closure of churches and the laity's deprivation of the sacraments, Archbishop Viganò is right to call it "a real unprecedented tragedy."[1] The drastic impact on the sacramental lives of the faithful cannot be exaggerated.

---

[1]   Kyle Hayes, "Ash Wednesday with Vigano, St Charles Borromeo, Hilarion, and the Coronavirus," *Inside the Vatican*, February 26, 2020,

1

Though the COVID-19 pandemic and the closure of churches around the world is unprecedented, there may be other situations where parishes and members of the faithful have to face local and individual emergencies that seriously disrupt normal sacramental life. Or we may face an emergency where circumstances make it impossible for us to reach a priest. It is a frightening prospect to face the possibility of being denied the sacraments during an emergency, especially if it is life-threatening. It is highly unlikely that secular authorities or first responders will appreciate the stress suffered by Catholics unable to receive the pastoral care of our priests, especially the anxiety caused by the possibility of not being able to receive Extreme Unction at the hour of death.

However, we can do much to reduce our own anxiety and stress if we find ourselves in such a situation by following two traditional devotional practices: the Act of Perfect Contrition and Spiritual Communion. As Bishop Schneider observed in his recent *Rorate Caeli* essay on the coronavirus, "In times of persecution, many Catholics were unable to receive Holy Communion in a sacramental way for long periods of time, but they made a Spiritual Communion with much spiritual benefit."[2]

Cardinal Johann Baptist Franzelin (1816–1886), the renowned dogmatic theologian and papal theologian during the First Vatican Council, once admitted, "If I were able

---

https://insidethevatican.com/news/newsflash/ash-wednesday-with-vigano-st-charles-borromeo-hilarion-and-the-coronavirus/.

[2]   Athanasius Schneider, "Op-Ed – Bishop Schneider: The Rite of Holy Communion in times of a pandemic," *Rorate Caeli*, February 28, 2020, https://rorate-caeli.blogspot.com/2020/02/op-ed-bishop-schneider-rite-of-holy.html.

to traverse the countryside preaching the divine word, my favorite sermon topic would be perfect contrition."[3]

Now is the time to recover the wisdom and practice of these traditional devotions. Under certain conditions, they will enable us to receive the forgiveness of our sins, and the marvelous benefit of Eucharistic graces if we are denied the sacraments and the pastoral care of our clergy—for example, due to self-isolation at home or quarantine in hospital.

Trust That God Wills to Save All Men

God, in his providence, has given the faithful these traditional means to receive absolution for our sins, under certain conditions, and the nourishment of Eucharistic graces because of his universal salvific will. As Sacred Scripture tells us, God does not wish the death of sinners but our conversion and life (see Ez 18:23), and he came into the world to save sinners and he wills to save all men (see 1 Tm 1:15; 2:4).

Our Lord has given special supernatural signification and effectiveness to the seven sacraments as unique signs and instruments of his saving grace that are necessary for salvation. However, St. Thomas Aquinas was clear that God has not restricted himself to these sacraments (ST III. 64. a2). In the Act of Perfect Contrition, which is intrinsically related to the sacrament of confession, and in Spiritual Communion, which is ardently focused on the sacrament of the Eucharist, we receive his saving grace. The economy of salvation is much more varied and multifaceted than many Catholics

---

[3]   J. De Driesch, "Perfect Contrition: The Golden Key to Paradise," *Pistrina Liturgica*, blog, http://pistrinaliturgica.blogspot.com/p/act-of-perfect-contrition.html.

nowadays assume, especially when we add in other sacramentals as well.

One of the signs of God's will to save all men that is inextricably bound up with the Act of Perfect Contrition and Spiritual Communion is individual conscience. God gives each person the faculty of conscience to guide us in our moral life so that we obey his law to do good and avoid sin. St. John Henry Newman writes that conscience is "a law, an authoritative voice" bidding us to "do certain things and avoid others."

> It *commands*, — that it praises, it blames, it promises, it threatens, it implies a future, and it witnesses the unseen. It is more than a man's own self. The man himself has not power over it, or only with extreme difficulty; he did not make it, he cannot destroy it. He may silence it in particular cases or directions, he may distort its enunciations, but he cannot, or it is quite the exception if he can, he cannot emancipate himself from it. He can disobey it, he may refuse to use it; but it remains. This is Conscience; and, from the nature of the case, its very existence carries on our minds to a Being exterior to ourselves; for else whence did it come? and to a Being superior to ourselves; else whence its strange, troublesome peremptoriness?[4]

For the Christian, baptized into the priestly, prophetic, and kingly life of Our Lord Jesus Christ, conscience attains its

---

[4]   Cardinal John Henry Newman, "Sermon 5. Dispositions for Faith," Parochial Sermons, http://www.newmanreader.org/works/occasions/sermon5.html.

true purpose because "it is a messenger from Him, who, both in nature and in grace, speaks to us behind a veil, and teaches and rules us by His representatives. Conscience is the aboriginal Vicar of Christ, a prophet in its informations, a monarch in its peremptoriness, a priest in its blessings and anathemas."[5]

Through conscience, the saving will of God seeks to bring all souls to heaven and avoid the eternal punishments of hell. God has given man his law of conscience to counter-balance his other great gift to us that most reflects his divine nature—the faculty of free will, which makes us capable of love. However, due to original sin, even when removed by Baptism, we remain easily attracted to evil, and as we well know, the fever of sin can deafen us to the voice of conscience. Cardinal Newman graphically explains how conscience can be obscured by the storms of sin:

> The reflection of sky and mountains in the lake is a proof that sky and mountains are around it, but the twilight, or the mist, or the sudden storm hurries away the beautiful image, which leaves behind it no memorial of what it was. Something like this are the Moral Law and the informations of Faith, as they present themselves to individual minds. Who can deny the existence of Conscience? who does not feel the force of its injunctions? but how dim is the illumination in which it is invested, and how feeble its influence, compared with that evidence of sight and touch which

---

5   Cardinal John Henry Newman, "Letter to the Duke of Norfolk," http://www.newmanreader.org/works/anglicans/volume2/gladstone/section5.html.

is the foundation of Physical Science! How easily can we be talked out of our clearest views of duty! how does this or that moral precept crumble into nothing when we rudely handle it! how does the fear of sin pass off from us, as quickly as the glow of modesty dies away from the countenance! and then we say, "It is all superstition."[6]

For these reasons, the discipline of a daily examination of conscience, informed by Sacred Scripture and the Church's teaching, is essential for the moral and spiritual life. It is even more important in emergency situations in which we find ourselves deprived of the sacrament of confession and the counsel of our priests. When we rely on acts of perfect contrition and spiritual communion it is vital that we practice daily examinations of conscience so as not to presume on the mercy of God but to receive his special graces through these devotions worthily.

The *Baltimore Catechism* recommends, "We may daily prepare for our judgment by a good examination of conscience, in which we will discover our sins and learn to fear the punishment they deserve" (1377). The catechism also explains, "We can make a good examination of conscience by calling to memory the commandments of God, the precepts of the Church, the seven capital sins, and the particular duties of our state in life, to find out the sins we have committed" (751). Before making your daily examination of conscience, ask the Holy Spirit to assist you in identifying

---

6   Cardinal John Henry Newman, "Christianity and Medial Science: An Address to the Students of Medicine," http://www.newman reader.org/works/idea/article10.html

your sins and to give you the grace of true contrition, and also ask for the grace to wholeheartedly trust in the mercy of God in order to avoid the pitfalls of scrupulosity. (A guide to an examination of conscience is provided at the end of this chapter.)

The Act of Perfect Contrition

As explained by the *Baltimore Catechism,* contrition "is sincere sorrow for having offended God, and hatred for the sins we have committed, with a firm purpose of sinning no more," and perfect contrition "is that which fills us with sorrow and hatred for sin, because it offends God, who is infinitely good in Himself and worthy of all love."

The Theology of the Act of Perfect Contrition

A number of the Church Fathers taught the efficacy of contrition for the remission of sin, including St John Chrysostom, who wrote, "As a fire which has taken possession of a forest, cleans it out thoroughly, so the fire of love, wheresoever it falls, takes away and blots out everything that could injure the divine seed, and purges the earth for the reception of that seed. Where love is, there all evils are taken away."[7]

Of course, the love that fires perfect contrition is the theological virtue of *caritas*, and so it is already an expression of the working of divine grace in one's life. The motivation

---

[7]   Joseph Pohle, *The Sacraments: A Dogmatic Treatise*, https://archive. org/stream/sacraments01pohluoft/sacraments01pohluoft_djvu. txt.

of *caritas* explains why perfect contrition is also sometimes called the *contrition of charity*.

One of the passages of Sacred Scripture that informs this understanding of perfect contrition is John 14:23, "Jesus answered him, 'Those who love me will keep my word, and my Father will love them, and we will come to them and make our home with them.'" The theological virtue of caritas leads those seeking Christian perfection to the contrition of charity and the consequent remission of sin that enables God to make his home in the soul.

St. Thomas Aquinas explicitly argued that perfect contrition could receive the pardon of sin outside of confession, "I answer that, Contrition can be considered in two ways, either as part of a sacrament, or as an act of virtue, and in either case it is the cause of the forgiveness of sin, but not in the same way" (ST Supplement. Q. v, a. 1.).

The Council of Trent went further by explaining the conditions that must be met for perfect contrition to remit sins, including mortal sins, outside of the sacrament of confession: "The Synod teaches moreover, that, although it sometimes happen that this contrition is perfect through charity, and reconciles man with God before this sacrament be actually received, the said reconciliation, nevertheless, is not to be ascribed to that contrition, independently of the desire of the sacrament which is included therein."[8]

Pope St. John Paul II's *Catechism of the Catholic Church* made this requirement of desiring sacramental confession as an element of perfect contrition explicit for the remission of

---

[8]   Council of Trent, Session xiv, chap 14, http://www.thecouncilof-trent.com/ch14.htm.

mortal sin: "[Perfect contrition] also obtains forgiveness of mortal sins if it includes the firm resolution to have recourse to sacramental confession as soon as possible" (CCC 1452).

Having said this, it is crucial that we understand the ability to make an act of perfect contrition is a grace of God for which we must earnestly pray. It also needs to be recognized that it is difficult for hardened sinners to make an act of perfect contrition. St. Alphonsus writes:

> Let us then, brethren, tremble at the thought of relapsing into sin, and let us beware of availing ourselves of the mercy of God to continue to offend him. "He", says St. Augustine, "who has promised pardon to all who repent of their sins, has promised repentance to no one". God has indeed promised pardon to all who repent of their sins, but he has not promised to any one the grace to repent of the faults which he has committed. Sorrow for sin is a pure gift of God; if he withholds it, how will you repent? And without repentance, how can you obtain pardon? Ah! the Lord will not allow himself to be mocked. "Be not deceived," says St. Paul, "God is not mocked." (Gal. vi. 7.) St. Isidore tells us, that the man who repeats the sin which he before detested, is not a penitent, but a scoffer of God's majesty.[9]

We must all guard against hardness of heart because Our Lord is angered and grieved when he finds hardened hearts

---

[9] St. Alphonsus de' Liguori, *The Sermons of St. Alphonsus Liguori: For All the Sundays of the Year* (Charlotte: TAN Books, 1982) Sermon XXI for Easter.

among those who should know better: "He looked around at them with anger; he was grieved at their hardness of heart" (Mk 3:5).

Those who choose to close their hearts to God, often through pride and thinking they know better than his Revelation, put themselves in a bad way because they deliberately resist God's grace. By so doing, they block true contrition and repentance, putting themselves in danger of mortal sin, and hell.

How to Make an Act of Perfect Contrition

In order to make an act of perfect contrition, the first thing to do is to be certain about the difference between imperfect contrition and perfect contrition. Father J. von den Driesch's very helpful booklet *Perfect Contrition: The Golden Key to Paradise* explains the differences. In summary, our contrition is imperfect if our motivation for repenting of our sins is due to fear of God because we think our sins will deny us heaven or will earn the punishment of purgatory or hell. Imperfect contrition originates from an imperfect love of God that puts our needs and desires and self-seeking love of favor before a true love of God.

We make an act of perfection contrition if we repent of our sins because when we think of God's greatness, his beauty, his love, his holiness, and are aware of how offensive our sins are to God and how they caused the sufferings of our Lord Jesus Christ on the cross. Perfect contrition originates from the theological virtue of caritas, a self-forgetful love of God that rejoices in God's holiness and redemptive love of sinful man, "For God so loved the world that he gave his only Son, so that everyone who believes in him may not perish but may have eternal life" (Jn 3:16).

Father J. von den Driesch explains the steps he considers necessary to make an act of perfect contrition:

1. Perfect Contrition is a grace from our merciful God, so sincerely ask him frequently throughout the day for this divine gift by repeating often, "My God, grant me perfect contrition for all my sins." God willingly gives this grace to those who ardently desire it.

2. In reality or imagination, kneel at the foot of a crucifix and meditate on Jesus's five precious wounds and his precious blood for a few moments and say to yourself, "Who, then, is nailed on this cross? It is Jesus, my God and my Savior. What does he suffer? His mangled body covered with wounds shows the ghastly torments. His soul is soaked with pains and insults. Why does he suffer? For men's sins and also for my own. In the midst of his bitterness, he remembers me, he suffers for me, he wishes to wipe away my sins."

3. Before the Crucified Christ, recall your sins, and forgetting for a moment heaven and hell, repent of them because they have brought our Lord to his sufferings on the cross. Promise him, that with his help, you will sin no more.

4. Recite, slowly and with fervor, an act of contrition that emphasizes the goodness of God and your love of Jesus. The following are well known or easy to memorize:

> O my God, because you are so good, I am very sorry that I have sinned against you, and by the help of your grace, I will not sin again. Amen.

> I love you, Jesus, my love, above all things, and I repent with my whole heart of having offended you. Never permit me to separate myself from you again, grant that I may love you always, and then do with me what you will. Amen.

5. Make a firm resolution to go to sacramental confession as soon as practically possible. If one is undergoing self-isolation or quarantine in hospital or the churches are closed as a consequence of the coronavirus, you should aim to go as soon as these restrictions are relaxed.

Father J. von den Driesch explains, "It's true that perfect contrition produces the same effects as confession, but it doesn't produce them independently of the sacrament of penance, since perfect contrition precisely supposes a firm purpose to confess the same sins that it has just pardoned."

It is important that you develop now the habit of making acts of perfect contrition throughout the day, and especially after an examination of conscience last thing at night. Then if you become critically ill or in danger of death without the assistance of a priest, you can readily make an act of perfect contrition sure in the knowledge that you have been forgiven your sins and that if you die, you will do so in a state of grace. If you don't die, then you can make a sacramental confession as soon as circumstances allow.

St. Maximilian Kolbe, OFM, wrote to his friends at the outbreak of war, when the German army invaded Poland, recommending that they immediately go to confession, but if that was already impossible, to make an act of perfect contrition: "Once again, December 8th is approaching, the Feast of The Immaculate Conception. Whoever can, should receive the Sacrament of Penance. Whoever cannot, because of prohibiting circumstances, should cleanse his soul by acts of perfect contrition: i.e., the sorrow of a loving child who does not consider so much the pain or the reward as he does the pardon from his father and mother to whom he has brought displeasure. Therefore, this desire is good: to purify our souls on the feast of her whose soul was never stained."[10]

Spiritual Communion

As explained in the *Baltimore Catechism,* Spiritual Communion is "an earnest desire to receive Communion in reality, by which desire we make all preparations and thanksgivings that we would make in case we really received the Holy Eucharist. Spiritual Communion is an act of devotion that must be pleasing to God and bring us blessings from Him."

The Theology of Spiritual Communion

St. Augustine is recognized as the first of the Church Fathers to touch upon Spiritual Communion in his homily on John 6:15-44: "Jesus answered and said to them, 'This is the work of God, that you believe in Him whom He has sent.' This is then to eat the meat, not that which perishes, but that which endures unto eternal life. To what purpose do you make ready teeth and stomach? Believe, and you have eaten already."[11]

---

[10]   Jonathan Conrad, "St. Maxamilian Kolbe: A final address to the knights of the Immaculata," *The Catholic Woodworker*, December 7, 2017, https://catholicwoodworker.com/blogs/reflections/st-max amilian-kolbe-a-final-address-to-the-knights-of-the-immaculata.

[11]   St. Augustine, Tractate 25 (John 6:15-44), https://www.newadvent. org/fathers/1701025.htm.

St. Augustine makes it clear that belief in the Blessed Sacrament is fundamental to Spiritual Communion, "Believe, and you have eaten already." For Augustine, faith and desire are inextricably linked—the greater our faith, the greater our desire for God, "The deeper our faith, the stronger our hope, the greater our desire, the larger will be our capacity to receive that gift, which is very great indeed" (Augustine's letter to Proba).

St. Thomas Aquinas further developed St. Augustine's thought by focusing on ardent desire for the Eucharist as necessary for Spiritual Communion: "The effect of the sacrament can be secured by every man if he receive it in desire, though not in reality. Consequently, just as some are baptized with the Baptism of desire, through their desire of baptism, before being baptized in the Baptism of water; so likewise some eat this sacrament spiritually ere they receive it sacramentally. Now this happens in two ways. First of all, from desire of receiving the sacrament itself, and thus are said to be baptized, and to eat spiritually, and not sacramentally, they who desire to receive these sacraments since they have been instituted" (ST III. q80. a1).

The Council of Trent presented St. Thomas Aquinas's understanding of spiritual communion as desire for the Blessed Sacrament as one of three ways of receiving Holy Communion: "For they have taught that some receive it sacramentally only, to wit sinners: others spiritually only, those to wit who eating in desire that heavenly bread which is set before them, are, by a lively faith which worketh by charity, made sensible of the fruit and usefulness thereof."[12]

---

[12]   Council of Trent, Concerning the Most Holy Sacrament of the

Since Trent, a number of popes have emphasized the importance of ardent desire for the Eucharist as essential to Spiritual Communion: "Christians—especially when they cannot easily receive holy communion—should do so at least by desire, so that with renewed faith, reverence, humility and complete trust in the goodness of the divine Redeemer, they may be united to Him in the spirit of the most ardent charity" (Pope Pius XII, *Mediator Dei*, 117). "It is good to *cultivate in our hearts a constant desire* for the sacrament of the Eucharist. This was the origin of the practice of 'spiritual communion'" (John Paul II, *Ecclesia de Eucharistia*, 34).

There are a number of ways that we can cultivate in our hearts a constant, ardent desire for the Blessed Sacrament. For example, while our churches remain open and before we may be self-isolating or under quarantine, we can commit to daily devout reception of Holy Communion and frequent Eucharistic Adoration. We can also read dogmatic and spiritual books on the Eucharist, such as *A Key to the Doctrine of the Eucharist* by Abbot Vonier, *God is Near Us: The Eucharist, The Heart of Life* by Joseph Cardinal Ratzinger, *Dominus Est: It Is the Lord!* by Bishop Athanasius Schneider, and *Corpus Christi: Holy Communion and the Renewal of the Church.*

How to Make a Spiritual Communion

There is some confusion concerning the nature of, and requirements for, Spiritual Communion. This has been caused by the contemporary recommendation, made by some clergyman, that individuals in a state of grave sin who

Eucharist, Chapter VIII.

cannot receive Holy Communion should instead make a Spiritual Communion during their participation in the Mass. For example, Pope Benedict XVI wrote in 2007, "Even in cases where it is not possible to receive sacramental communion, participation at Mass remains necessary, important, meaningful and fruitful. In such circumstances it is beneficial to cultivate a desire for full union with Christ through the practice of spiritual communion" (*Sacramentum Caritatis* 55).

This is a different type of "spiritual communion" than the traditional devotion of Spiritual Communion, which requires that "we make all preparations and thanksgivings that we would make in case we really received the Holy Eucharist" (*Baltimore Catechism*). Such preparations would necessarily include the requirement of confession if we were aware of being in a state of mortal sin. Servant of God Felice Capello, SJ, wrote in his *Tractatus Canonico-Moralis*, "He who is in mortal sin" must at least "repent in his heart if he wishes to spiritually communicate profitably."[13] The necessity of being in a state of grace was also explained by Fr. Francis D. Costa, SSS: "The person [making an act of Spiritual Communion] must be in the state of grace, since this is a necessary condition for Holy Communion, and also because this desire is essentially an act of love of Christ in the Blessed Sacrament."[14]

---

[13]   Mary Anne Hackett, "Can Someone in Mortal Sin Receive Communion?" CatholicCitizens.org, https://catholiccitizens.org/views/58636/can-someone-in-mortal-sin-receive-communion/.

[14]   Michael D. Griffin, *The Nature and Effect of Spiritual Communion*, http://ejournals.bc.edu/ojs/index.php/ctsa/article/download/2463/2092.

It follows from this that if we are unable to have recourse to sacramental confession due to self-isolation or quarantine, we can prepare ourselves to undertake the devotion of Spiritual Communion by making an act of perfect contrition.

St. Leonard of Port Maurice, OFM, (1676–1751) recommended the following way of making a spiritual communion in his book *The Hidden Treasure: Or The Immense Excellence of the Holy Sacrifice of the Mass*. Though his recommendations were written for Spiritual Communion during Mass when the priest communicates, they can be adapted to Spiritual Communion outside of the Mass.

- At the moment when the priest is about to receive Holy Communion, at the same time, "excite in your heart an act of sincere contrition and humbly strike your breast in acknowledgment of your unworthiness to receive so great a grace." If self-isolating or in quarantine, bring to mind in your imagination the sacred words and actions of the Mass, such as the consecration and elevation of the Host and Chalice or the priest's communion. Know that as you imagine this in your mind's eye, somewhere in the world a priest is offering up the sacrifice of the Mass. Or if possible, participate in the Mass virtually—for example, through the internet or TV.

- Make all those acts of faith, humility, sorrow, adoration, love, and desire that you usually express through prayers before Holy Communion.

- Ardently desire, with earnest longing, to receive "your adorable Jesus who has deigned to veil

Himself in the Sacrament for your spiritual and temporal welfare." Imagine that the Mother of God, or some one of your patron saints, administers the adorable particle to you; think that you are actually receiving it, and after embracing Jesus in your heart, say to him over and over again with heart-felt words dictated by love, such as the following prayer: "My Jesus, I believe that Thou art present in the Blessed Sacrament. I love Thee above all things and I desire Thee in my soul. Since I cannot now receive Thee sacramentally, come at least spiritually into my heart. As though Thou wert already there, I embrace Thee and unite myself wholly to Thee; permit not that I should ever be separated from Thee. Amen" (St. Alphonsus Liguori).

• After moments of silent adoration, make all those acts of faith, humility, love, thanksgiving, and offering that you usually express through prayers after Holy Communion.

One of the wonderful benefits of Spiritual Communion is that you can make it many times during the day and night. St. Maximilian Kolbe undertook this devotion at least once every quarter of an hour. St. Pio of Pietrelcina (Padre Pio) recommended receiving our Lord in Spiritual Communion throughout the day during one's various occupations. To encourage this devotion he taught, "Fly with your spirit before the tabernacle, when you can't stand before it bodily, and there pour out the ardent longings of your soul and embrace the Beloved of souls, even more than if you had been permitted to receive him sacramentally."[15]

It will be a great consolation to receive Eucharistic graces through Spiritual Communion if we are unable to receive Holy Communion due to self-isolation, quarantine, or the closure of churches for weeks on end. As St. Teresa of Jesus advised, "When you do not receive communion and you do not attend Mass, you can make a spiritual communion, which is a most beneficial practice; by it the love of God will be greatly impressed on you."[16]

St. Jean-Marie Vianney recommended Spiritual Communion as a means to keeping our faith aflame with love: "When we feel the love of God growing cold, let us instantly make a Spiritual Communion. When we cannot go to the church, let us turn towards the tabernacle; no wall can shut us out from the good God."

Though these traditional devotions of Perfect Contrition and Spiritual Communion really come into their own when we are denied the sacraments due to times of emergency, it is best to make them a daily practice even when we remain free to attend our parish churches. Cultivating these habits will make it easier for us to avail ourselves of their benefits when caught up in the middle of a crisis.

---

[15]   Vinny Flynn, *7 Secrets of the Eucharist* (Stockbridge: Mercysong, 2006), 89.

[16]   *The Way of Perfection*, ch. 35.

More Devotions for Acts of Perfect Contrition and Spiritual Communion

St. Don Bosco's Examination of Conscience

Though this was composed by St. Don Bosco to assist boys and young men, it is a helpful examination of conscience for times of emergency due to its brevity and thoroughness.

Place yourself in the presence of God and earnestly ask his help to make an examination of conscience well:

My Lord Jesus Christ, Redeemer of my soul, I throw myself at Your feet, begging You to have pity on me. Enlighten me with Your grace, that I may now see my sins as I shall see them when I come before You to be judged. Grant, O Lord, that I may detest them with true sorrow, and that I may obtain the pardon of them all, through the infinite merits of Your Most Precious Blood shed for me upon the Cross. Most Holy Virgin, all You Saints of God, pray for me, that I may make a good confession. Amen.

Sins Against God

Not saying morning and night prayers; missing Mass on Sundays or holy days of obligation; irreverence in church; taking God's name in vain; cursing; swearing; being ashamed of your religion; bad use of God's gifts and sacraments; superstitious practices.

Sins Against Your Neighbor

Disrespect and disobedience to your parents, priest, teachers, elders; stealing; cheating; wasting time, your own or your employer's; bad judgement; backbiting; calumny;

detraction; jealousy; feelings of revenge and wishing harm should come to anyone; telling lies; bad talk or immodest acts with others; giving scandal in this way or by your bad conduct in other ways; leading others into sin in any way whatsoever.

Sins Against Yourself

Greediness; obstinacy; sullenness; anger; impatience; impure thoughts or acts; going into occasions of sin; eating meat on Fridays.

Prayer to Your Guardian Angel to Assist Your Spiritual Communion

O Holy Angel at my side,
Go to Church for me,
Kneel in my place, at Holy Mass,
Where I desire to be.

At Offertory, in my stead,
Take all I am and own,
And place it as a sacrifice
Upon the Altar Throne.

At Holy Consecration's bell,
Adore with Seraph's love,
My Jesus hidden in the Host,
Come down from Heaven above.

Then pray for those I dearly love,
And those who cause me grief,

That Jesus' Blood may cleanse all hearts,
And suff'ring souls relieve.

And when the priest Communion takes,
Oh, bring my Lord to me,
That His sweet Heart may rest on mine,
And I His temple be.

Pray that this Sacrifice Divine,
May mankind's sins efface;
Then bring me Jesus' blessing home,
The pledge of every grace. Amen

Cardinal Merry del Val's Prayer of Spiritual Communion

At Your feet, O my Jesus,
I prostrate myself and I offer You
repentance of my contrite heart,
which is humbled in its nothingness
and in Your holy presence.
I adore You in the Sacrament of Your love,
the ineffable Eucharist.
I desire to receive You
into the poor dwelling that my heart offers You.
While waiting for the happiness of sacramental
    communion,
I wish to possess You in spirit.
Come to me, O my Jesus,
since I, for my part, am coming to You!

May Your love embrace my whole being in life and in
   death.
I believe in You,
I hope in You,
I love You. Amen.

St. Thomas More's Act of Perfect Contrition and Spiritual Communion

St. Thomas More composed this prayer during his imprison-
ment in the Tower of London after he had been told that he
had been condemned to death.

Give me, good Lord, a longing to be with You, not for
the avoiding of the calamities of this wretched world,
nor so much for the avoiding of the pains of purgatory, nor of the pains of hell neither, nor so much for
the attaining of the joys of heaven in respect of mine
own commodity, as even, for a very love to You.

Take from me, good Lord, this lukewarm fashion
. . . and this dulness in praying to You. And give me
warmth, delight, and quickness in thinking upon You.
And give me Your grace to long for Your holy sacraments, and specially to rejoice in the presence of Your
very blessed body, sweet Saviour Christ, in the holy
sacrament of the altar, and duly to thank You for Your
gracious visitation therewith, and at that high memorial with tender compassion to remember and consider
Your most bitter passion.

Make us all, good Lord, virtually participant of
that holy sacrament this day, and every day. Make us

all lively members, sweet Saviour Christ, of Your holy mystical body, Your Catholic Church. Amen.[17]

St. Thomas More's Advice on Recollection After Receiving Communion

The great English martyr also composed this advice to foster recollection after the reception of sacramental Communion, but it is equally useful for Spiritual Communion.

> Now when we have received our Lord and have Him inside our body, let us not then leave Him alone as we get involved in other things, forgetting to look to Him anymore. For anyone who would serve a guest in such a way would have little sense!
>
> Instead, let all our concern be focused on Him. Let us by devout prayer talk to Him, by devout meditation talk with Him. Let us say with the prophet: "I will hear what our Lord will speak within me" (Ps 85:9). If we set aside all other things and attend to Him, He will not fail to inspire us, to speak to us such things within us that will lead to the great spiritual comfort and profit of our soul. Having received the Blessed Sacrament, we have a special time of prayer. For He who made us, who redeemed us, whom we have offended, who will judge us, who will either damn us or save us, has because of His great goodness become our guest. He is personally present within us—and He has done

---

[17]   Thomas Edward Bridgett, *The Wisdom and Wit of Blessed Thomas More* (London: Burns and Oates, Ltd., 1892), 94-97.

that for no other purpose but to be sought for pardon so that He can save us.

Let us not lose this time, therefore, nor allow this occasion to slip by. For we can hardly tell whether we will ever get in to church again or not.[18]

Prayers Before Spiritual Communion[19]

Though these prayers were composed as preparation for, and thanksgiving after, sacramental Communion, they are also suitable for Spiritual Communion.

Prayer For Help

O God, help me make a good Communion. Mary, my dearest mother, pray to Jesus for me. My dear Angel Guardian, lead me to the altar of God.

Act of Humility

My God, I confess that I am a poor sinner; I am not worthy to receive the Body and Blood of Jesus, on account of my sins. Lord, I am not worthy to receive you under my roof; but only say the word, and my soul will be healed.

Act of Sorrow

My God, I detest all the sins of my life. I am sorry for them, because they have offended you, my God, you are so good.

---

[18] St. Thomas More, *Treatise: To Receive the Blessed Body of Our Lord*, http://archive.ccwatershed.org/media/pdfs/18/01/21/15-59-10_0.pdf.

[19] *A Simple Prayer Book* (London: Catholic Truth Society, 1974), 23-26.

I resolve never to commit sin any more. My good God, pity me, have mercy on me, forgive me.

Act of Adoration

O Jesus, great God, present on the Altar, I bow down before you, I adore you.

Act of Love and Desire

Jesus, I love you. I desire with all my heart to receive you. Jesus, come into my poor soul, and give me your Flesh to eat and your Blood to drink. Give me your whole Self, Body, Blood, Soul and Divinity, that I may live for ever with you.

Prayers After Spiritual Communion
Act of Adoration

O Jesus, my God, my Creator, I adore you, because from your hands I came and with you I am to be happy for ever.

Act of Humility

O Jesus, I am not worthy to receive you, and yet you come to me that my poor heart may learn of you to be meek and humble.

Act of Love

Jesus, I love you; I love you with all my heart. You know that I love you, and wish to love you daily more and more.

Act of Thanksgiving

My good Jesus, I thank you with all my heart. You know that I love you, and wish to love you daily more and more.

Act of Offering

O Jesus, receive my poor offering. Jesus, you have given yourself to me, and now let me give myself to you:

I give you my body, that it may be chaste and pure.

I give you my soul, that it may be free from sin.

I give you my heart, that it may always love you.

I give you every breath that I shall breathe, and especially my last, I give you myself in life and in death, that I may be yours for ever and ever.

Remember the words of Jesus *Ask and you shall receive.*

Pray for Others

O Jesus, have mercy on your holy Church; take care of it.

O Jesus, have pity on poor sinners, and save them from hell.

O Jesus, bless my father, my mother, my brothers and sisters, and all I ought to pray for, as your Heart knows how to bless them.

O Jesus, have pity on the poor souls in purgatory and give them eternal rest.

Pray for Yourself

O Jesus, wash away my sins in your Precious Blood.

O Jesus, the struggle against temptation is not yet finished. My Jesus, when temptation comes near me, make me strong against it. In the moment of temptation may I always say: "My Jesus, mercy! Mary, help!"

O Jesus, may I lead a good life; may I die a happy death. May I receive you before I die. May I say when I am dying: "Jesus, Mary and Joseph, I give you my heart and soul."

Listen now for a moment to Jesus Christ; perhaps he has something to say to you. Answer Jesus in your heart, and tell him all your troubles. Then say:

Jesus, I am going away for a time, but I trust not without you. You are with me by your grace. I resolve never to leave you by mortal sin. Give me grace to persevere. Amen.

What to Do When Suffering Life-Threatening Situations Without a Priest

Emergencies, such as the COVID-19 coronavirus pandemic, bring the prospect of death into much sharper focus. The illusion that we will live to an old age, that made death seem a far-distant threat, is ripped away, leaving us to face the truth of our mortality. A car accident, a plane crash, a violent assault, a heart attack, a stroke, a life-threatening virus. Our well-ordered, predictable lives are turned on their heads by the chaos and threat of unexpected emergencies. A world that seemed safe and familiar suddenly becomes dangerous and alien. It can shock us to the core of our being.

In our imaginations, we envisage our future deathbeds attended by priests and family, but unexpected events can rob us of such peaceful deaths. The one thing the COVID-19 pandemic has taught us is that events can overwhelm our plans for the future. The prospect of dying without the assistance of priests rightly concerns many of us. We may feel a deep anxiety about being left alone to endure the tribulations of dying without our spiritual fathers or family.

In these circumstances, familiarity and practice of two traditional devotions will help us face death with greater peace of mind, calmness, and composure, enabling us to prepare to die with Christian hope. These two traditional devotions are the *Ars Moriendi* and the *Bona Mors*—the art of dying and prayers for a happy death. Even if we are young and healthy, we would all benefit from these two devotions that help us live life from the perspective of Eternal Life.

The Risen Christ Transfigures Death

It is from Our Lord's conquest of death and his defeat of Satan that the Art of Dying Well and the Prayers for a Happy Death derive their power to transfigure our experience of death. They rob death of its sting by taking us deeper into our baptismal participation in his death and resurrection (see Rom 6:4).

Death is the dire consequence of our first parents' sin that expresses the "wrath and indignation of God."[20] Death is also the baleful manifestation of our captivity to the devil who "has the power of death" (Hb 2:14). As St. Augustine explains:

> Wherefore we must say that the first men were indeed so created, that if they had not sinned, they would not have experienced any kind of death; but that, having become sinners, they were so punished with death, that whatsoever sprang from their stock should also be punished with the same death. For nothing else could be born of them than that which they themselves had been. Their nature was deteriorated in proportion to the greatness of the condemnation of their sin, so that

---

[20]   Council of Trent's Decree on Original Sin, 1; see also Gn 2:17.

> what existed as punishment in those who first sinned,
> became a natural consequence in their children.[21]

For these reasons alone it is understandable why individuals have a natural dread of death, even if they are unaware of the supernatural origin of this fear. As death approaches, we will all have to contend with this aboriginal dread, which—without the fortification of Christian faith and sacramental life—can be overwhelming.

The resurrection of Our Lord changes everything. As St. Thomas Aquinas puts it, the Resurrection is the "beginning and exemplar of all good things" (ST III q.53 a.1, ad 3). "I am the resurrection and the life. Those who believe in me, even though they die, will live, and everyone who lives and believes in me will never die" (Jn 11:25–26).

Through the humanity assumed by the Son of God, Christ bore through his dying on the cross, the punishment of God's wrath and indignation and freed humanity from captivity to the devil's power of death. "'Death has been swallowed up in victory.' 'Where, O death, is your victory! Where, O death, is your sting?' . . . But thanks be to God, who gives us the victory through our Lord Jesus Christ" (1 Cor 15:54–55, 57).

Our Lord's victory over death is why one of the unique characteristics of Christianity is joy in the face of suffering and death. As St. Teresa of Calcutta (Mother Teresa) puts it, "Never let anything so fill you with sorrow as to make you forget the joy of Christ risen." St. Paul expresses the

---

[21]   St. Augustine, *The City of God*, Book XIII, Chap. 1, https://www.newadvent.org/fathers/120113.htm.

joy he found in suffering for Our Lord, "And not only that, but we also boast in our sufferings, knowing that suffering produces endurance, and endurance produces character, and character produces hope, and hope does not disappoint us, because God's love has been poured into our hearts through the Holy Spirit that has been given to us" (Rom 5:3–5).

St. Paul describes this Christian joy in suffering as a grace of the Holy Spirit, "And you became imitators of us and of the Lord, for in spite of persecution you received the word with joy inspired by the Holy Spirit" (1 Thes 1:6). St. John Chrysostom, who died a martyr's death, also speaks of the joy found in suffering: "One can be joyful despite lashes and blows, when these are accepted in the cause of Christ. A feature of the joy of the Holy Spirit is that it causes an uncontainable happiness to grow even out of affliction and sorrow. . . . In the natural course of events afflictions do not produce joy: joy is the privilege of those who accept sufferings for Jesus Christ's sake: it is one of the good things bestowed by the Holy Spirit."[22]

A great example of the power of Christian joy is the twentieth-century martyr Blessed Karl Leisner. Amidst the cruel deprivations and inhumanity of the Dachau concentration camp, Karl Leisner was known for his joy, even though he suffered from tuberculosis. Fr. Otto Pies, SJ, wrote an account of Blessed Karl Leisner participating as a deacon in a clandestine celebration of the Christmas Vigil Mass with fellow inmates:

---

[22]   *The Navarre Bible: Thessalonians and Pastoral Letters* (Dublin: Four Court Press, 2005), 21.

Radiant and blissful, he chanted the Gospel of the good news of great joy "which shall be to all the people". It was an unforgettable experience for many of us to observe with what a deep, moving devotion and joy the deacon discharged the duties of his holy office on this eve of Christmas. There reigned a childlike rejoicing among the participants in spite of the surrounding reality. Seldom had one seen men as joyful and happy as these prisoners who in blissful joy embraced each other and wished each other good luck in the darkness of the camp streets or in the poverty of their rooms. The most joyous among the joy-filled men was Karl Leisner; for he had been so near to the Divine Child in the form of bread and wine and had been permitted to celebrate the mystery of love with him.[23]

St. Thomas Aquinas explains that the Christian is joyful to bear the sufferings of this life because they have been transformed by Christ as the penitential means to enter into the glory of eternal life: "A person who hopes for something and strives eagerly to attain it is ready to endure all kinds of difficulty and distress. Thus, for example, a sick person, if he is eager to be healthy, is happy to take the bitter medicine which will cure him. Therefore, one sign of the ardent hope that is ours thanks to Christ is that we glory, not only in the hope of future glory, but also in the afflictions which we suffer in order to attain it."[24]

---

[23] Otto Pies, *The Victory of Father Karl* (London: Victor Gollancz, 1957), 131–32.

[24] *The Navarre Bible: Romans & Galatians* (Dublin: Four Court Press, 2005), 86–87.

Facing death without the assistance of a priest or our family, we can ask the Holy Spirit for the fruit of his joy as we return to God.

The Art of Dying Well

In his famous book-length meditation on the art of dying well, St. Robert Bellarmine begins by setting out the fundamental Christian hope that energizes this devotion. He explains that, though death cannot be considered a good in itself because it originates in sin, God in his providential wisdom has "so seasoned it . . . that from death many blessings arise." The greatest blessing being that it can become the gate from the prison of this earthly life to the Kingdom of God. Therefore, Bellarmine's starting point for the art of dying well is that through the grace of Christ, "death to the good man seems not horrible, but sweet; not terrible, but lovely." This attitude to death is exemplified by St. Paul when he writes, "For to me, living is Christ and dying is gain" (Phil 1:21).

Professor Eamon Duffy, in his seminal book on pre-Reformation Catholicism in England,[25] sets out the purpose and elements of the medieval manuals that guided the priests in their preparation of the mortally sick for death. These pastoral practices informed the structure and content of the *Ars Moriendi*. It included the following elements:

First. The priest presented the dying person with the crucifix, which was held before their face to reassure them "that in the image they may adore their redeemer and have

---

25   Eamon Duffy, *The Stripping of the Altars* (New Haven: Yale University Press, 1992).

in mind his passion, which he endured for their sins."[26] The English mystic Juliana of Norwich described the effect of this presentation of the crucifix on her as she lay seriously ill. "The parson set the cross before my face and said: Daughter, I have brought you the image of your savior. Look at it and take comfort from it, in reverence of him who died for you and me."[27]

Second. The *Ars Moriendi* emphasized the comfort to be gained by meditating on the Crucified Christ by using a popular meditation of St. Bernard. This meditation described Jesus on the cross with his arms extended, his head bowed, to embrace and kiss the sinner, and his side wound exposed to reveal his burning love. Its origin was a mystical vision of St. Bernard during which he saw the Crucified Christ lean down from the cross to embrace and support him. The compassion of the Crucified Christ towards the sinner was a common theme in the writings of St. Bernard: "The world rages, the flesh is heavy, and the devil lays his snares, but I do not fall, for my feet are planted on firm rock. I may have sinned gravely. My conscience would be distressed, but it would not be in turmoil, for I would recall the wounds of the Lord: He was wounded for our iniquities. What sin is there so deadly that it cannot be pardoned by the death of Christ? And so, if I bear in mind this strong, effective remedy, I can never again be terrified by the malignancy of sin."[28]

Third. It is within the context of Our Lord's death on the cross for our sins and his compassion for sinners that the

---

26   Ibid., 314.
27   Julian of Norwich, *Showings* (New York: Paulist Press, 1978), 128.
28   The Divine Office, Wednesday in the 3rd week of ordinary time.

priest questioned the dying person to encourage a spirit of honest repentance—one that trusts solely in the redemptive sufferings of Christ. As St. Augustine wrote, "However innocent your life may have been, no Christian ought to venture to die in any other state than that of the penitent."[29] Eamon Duffy explains that the purpose of this interrogation was to bring the dying Christian to the knowledge of their condition, even if it disturbed and frightened them; for it was better to trouble the dying with wholesome fear and dread than allow them to fall into damnation. The purpose of this was to evoke from the dying a declaration of faith in Christ and true repentance of their sins.

Fourth. Such a declaration of faith and repentance was to strengthen the dying person to withstand the final assault of the devil: "The deathbed is the center of an epic struggle for the soul of the Christian, in which the devil bent all his strength to turn the soul from Christ and His cross to self-loathing or self-reliance. Against these temptations the cross and the armies of the redeemed were marshalled to assist the dying Christian. The bedroom became a crowded battlefield centered on the last agonies of the man or woman in the bed."[30]

Following the principle of being forewarned is to be forearmed, the Ars Moriendi prepared the Christian soul to identify and endure five temptations from the devil as they died:

- Temptation against Faith. At the last moment, the

---

29   Richard Challoner, *The Garden of the Soul.*
30   Duffy, *The Stripping of the Altars*, 317.

dying Christian will be tempted to apostasy, against which they must pray for the virtue of faith and steadfastly renew their baptismal faith.

- Temptation to despair. The devil tempts the dying to despair of the forgiveness of God by presenting the deadly sins as unpardonable, which must be countered by prayer for the virtue of hope in God's forgiveness.

- Temptation to angry impatience. The dying person is tempted to reject God's permissive will for them to endure sickness and death, expressed through impatience and frustration with one's situation and against one's carers. This is to be countered with the deliberate practice of patience, forbearance, and charity.

- Temptation to pride. Faced with declining powers and lack of control, the dying person is tempted by the devil to desperately cling onto a false sense of security by focusing on one's past achievements and social status. Instead of sinking into this illusion, the Christian must embrace an honest assessment of one's sins and cultivate humility expressed as total reliance on God.

- Temptation to an avaricious attachment to people and possessions. As one faces the extreme poverty of being dead, the devil will tempt us to cling to our relationships and possessions. To counter this illusion, the dying person must seek detachment, accepting the stripping of faculties and familiar securities, abandoning oneself to God, "Father, into your hands I commend my spirit" (Lk 23:46).

Fifth. The Ars Moriendi fortified and encouraged the Christian facing battle with the devil by reassuring them of the active presence and direct assistance of angels and saints. It reminded them that they were in the company of great sinners who converted to become great saints, such as St. Peter, St. Mary Magdalene, St. Dismas, the good thief, and St. Paul. In his epic poem *The Dream of Gerontius,* St. John Henry Newman vividly portrays the role played by our guardian angel at the hour of death, assisting the soul to God's judgement seat and protecting it from the final assaults of the demons.

Sixth. The family and friends played an important role at the moment the dying person expired by praying out loud prayers of commendation. As it states in the rubrics for the Prayers for the Dying set out in the traditional Roman Missal, "When the moment of death draws near, then all who stand at the bedside should pray with great earnestness, and upon their knees. If the dying person is able, he should say: Jesus, Jesus, Jesus. If he cannot, someone standing near, or the priest himself, should do so in a clear voice."[31]

An Ars Moriendi for Times of Emergency

Faced with the prospect of being quarantined in a hospital and deprived of the assistance of our priests and family at the hour of death, it is prudent to practice the art of dying well as a frequent devotion. The following is based on the

---

[31] *The Small Ritual: Being Extracts from the Rituale Romanum in Latin & in English* (London: Burns & Oates, 1964), 145.

traditional practice, adapted to the circumstances of death on one's own:

1. Look at a crucifix, or bring one to mind in your imagination, and adore your redeemer. Recollect his passion, which he endured for your sins.

2. Meditate on the compassion of your Savior towards you as a sinner. Imagine Jesus on the cross with his arms extended, his head bowed, embracing and supporting you, helping you face your sins.

3. Undertake a general examination of your conscience, asking the Holy Spirit to uncover the sins of your life. Ask for the grace of honest repentance, not making excuses or rationalizations of sinful actions, trusting solely in the redemptive sufferings of Christ. If you are aware of any mortal or serious sins, ask for the grace to make an act of perfect contrition, which will absolve even these sins in the absence of a priest (under certain conditions).

4. Expect to undergo the final assault of the devil as you die. Pray for grace as follows:

> Against apostasy—pray for the virtue of faith and reaffirm your baptismal faith.
> Against despair over sins—pray for the virtue of hope in God's forgiveness.
> Against anger at dying—pray for the virtue of charity so as to practice patience.
> Against clinging to pride—pray for humility and total reliance on God.

Against attachment to this life—pray for detachment and abandonment to God's will.

At the moment of temptation, always also say, "My Jesus, mercy! Mary, help!"

5. Pray for the assistance of your guardian angel and the communion of saints, especially St. Peter, St. Mary Magdalene, St. Dismas (the Good Thief), and St. Paul.

6. Unable to receive Viaticum due to the absence of a priest, make a Spiritual Communion by ardently longing to receive Holy Communion.

7. At the moment of death, pray out loud or in your heart, "Jesus, Jesus, Jesus" or "Jesus, Mary, and Joseph, I give you my heart and my soul; Jesus, Mary, and Joseph, assist me in my last agony. Jesus, Mary, and Joseph, may I breathe forth my spirit in peace with you. Amen."

Prayers for a Happy Death

At a time when sudden, unexpected death was a common reality of everyday life, it was a popular devotional practice for Catholics to pray for a happy death. In the seventeenth century, the Jesuits, with papal approval, founded the Bona Mors Confraternity to "prepare its members by a well-regulated life to die in peace with God."[32] Richard Challoner, the eminent English bishop during the Penal Times, included in his devotional book *The Garden of the Soul*, *Litanies for a Happy Death*, composed by "a Young Lady, who

---

[32]   *Catholic Encyclopedia*, s.v., "The Bona Mors Confraternity," https://www.newadvent.org/cathen/02648a.htm.

at ten years of age, was converted to the Catholic Faith, and died at eighteen, in the odor of sanctity" (p. 46).

St. Joseph, Patron of a Happy Death

An essential element of these devotions is the veneration of St. Joseph, as the patron of a happy death. This association of St. Joseph with the hour of death can be traced back to a fifth century devotional text *The Life of Joseph the Carpenter*, which imagines St. Joseph, in fear of impending death, being comforted by Jesus. Joseph says to Jesus, "All hail! My well-beloved son. Indeed, the agony and fear of death have already environed me; but as soon as I heard Your voice, my soul was at rest. O Jesus of Nazareth! Jesus, my Savior! Jesus, the deliverer of my soul! Jesus, my protector! Jesus! O sweetest name in my mouth, and in the mouth of all those that love it! O eye which sees, and ear which hears, hear me! I am Your servant; this day I most humbly reverence You, and before Your face I pour out my tears. You are altogether my God."[33]

Since the fifth century, a popular depiction of the death of St. Joseph shows him embraced by Jesus and Mary, the perfect image of a happy death. St. Alphonsus Liguori presents St. Joseph's death as the ideal Christian death: "And by that assistance which Jesus and Mary gave thee at death, I beg of thee to protect me in a special way at the hour of my death, so that dying, assisted by thee, in the company of Jesus and

---

[33] "The History of Joseph the Carpenter," New Advent, https://www.newadvent.org/fathers/0805.htm.

Mary, I may go to thank thee in paradise, and in thy company praise my God for all eternity. Amen."[34]

Father Francis Filas, SJ, observed that "no deathbed scene could ever have been attended by witnesses who were more consoling."[35]

Various popes have promoted veneration of St. Joseph as the patron of a happy death. In his prayer to St. Joseph, Pope Leo XIII wrote, "Shield us ever under thy patronage, that, following thine example and strengthened by thy help, we may live a holy life, die a happy death, and attain to everlasting bliss in Heaven. Amen."[36] Pope Benedict XV encouraged the faithful to invoke St. Joseph on Wednesdays as the patron of a happy death. He urged the world's bishops to promote devotion to him: "Particularly, since he is thought to be the most effective protector of the dying people, as he died with the attendance of Jesus and Mary, it will be up to the Holy Shepherds to introduce and to sponsor, with all the prestige of their authority, those devout prayers which were instituted for invoking S. Joseph for the dying people, like that one 'of the happy death', of the 'Transit of S. Joseph for everyday agonizing.'"[37]

---

[34]   *Favorite Prayers to St. Joseph* (Charlotte: TAN Books, 1994).

[35]   Louise Perrotta, Patron of a "Happy Death:" A Special Role for St. Joseph, *The Word Among Us*, https://wau.org/resources/article/re_patron_of_a_happy_death/.

[36]   Pope Leo XIII, *Quanquam Pluries*, http://www.vatican.va/content/leo-xiii/en/encyclicals/documents/hf_l-xiii_enc_15081889_quamquam-pluries.html.

[37]   Pope Benedict XV, "Proclamation of Saint Joseph patron of the universal," Church https://digilander.libero.it/monast/giuseppe/inglese/benedetto.htm.

St. Joseph, Terror of Demons

In light of the devil's final assault at the deathbed, it is also sensible to invoke the assistance of St. Joseph, the Terror of demons, as he is described in his litany. Entrusted by God with the virtues and graces to protect the Son of God and the Blessed Virgin Mary, St. Joseph rightly terrifies the devil and his hordes. As the foster father of Jesus, to whose authority Jesus was subject (see Lk 2:51), and as the chaste spouse of the Mother of God, St. Joseph holds a special place in heaven. Father Antony Patrigani writes about St. Joseph's special place in heaven in *A Manual of Practical Devotion to the Glorious Patriarch St. Joseph* (1885):

> Lucifer is aware of this, and hence it is that with fear and trembling he approaches the bed of a dying person who, during life, had been a true servant of St. Joseph. He knows that our Divine Savior, in order to reward His great saint for having saved Him from the sword of Herod and a temporal death, has given him the special privilege of preserving those dying persons who, during life, looked up to him as their protector, from the power of the devil and eternal death . . . [they] are sure to find beneath his wings their best security against the arts of Satan at that tremendous crisis, when his fury is raised to its highest pitch at the prospect of his prey about to escape from him forever.[38]

---

[38] Antony Patrignani, *A Manual of Practical Devotion to St. Joseph* (Charlotte: TAN Books, 1982).

A Bona Mors for Times of Emergency

While there is still time, make these prayers for a happy death your daily practice so that if you get caught up in an emergency and develop serious, life-threatening complications, they will have already become part of your daily prayer life. In this way, you can be confident that through the protection and intercession of St. Joseph you will defeat the final temptations of the devil and be granted the grace of a happy death.

Make an Act of Consecration to St. Joseph

> O dearest St. Joseph, I consecrate myself to your honor and give myself to you, that you may always be my father, my protector and my guide in the way of salvation. Obtain for me a greater purity of heart and fervent love of the interior life. After your example may I do all my actions for the greater glory of God, in union with the Divine Heart of Jesus and the Immaculate Heart of Mary. O Blessed St. Joseph, pray for me, that I may share in the peace and joy of your holy death. Amen.

Often Pray This Prayer to St. Joseph for a Happy Death

> O Glorious St. Joseph, behold I choose thee today for my special patron in life and at the hour of my death. Preserve and increase in me the spirit of prayer and fervor in the service of God. Remove far from me every kind of sin; obtain for me that my death may not

come upon me unawares, but that I may have time to confess my sins sacramentally and to bewail them with a most perfect understanding and a most sincere and perfect contrition, in order that I may breathe forth my soul into the hands of Jesus and Mary. Amen.

Pray St. Luigi Guanella's Universal Prayer for the Dying

Glorious Saint Joseph, adoptive father of the Son of God and true husband of the Holy Virgin Mary, pray for us and for our brothers that agonize in this day (or night).

To conclude, in normal circumstances it would be wise to make the art of dying well and prayers for a happy death a frequent practice because we each have to face the hour of death. But emergencies like the COVID-19 pandemic serve a good purpose of reminding us of the necessity to take up these devotions in order to prepare for the possibility that we will face our deathbeds without the assistance of priests and family. If we have to face such a death, we can be sure of the protection of St. Joseph and the consoling presence of Our Lord and the Blessed Virgin Mary. Let us make this prayer of Padre Pio our own:

It is getting late and death approaches, I fear the darkness, the temptations, the dryness, the cross, the sorrows. O how I need You, my Jesus, in this night of exile! Stay with me Lord, because at the hour of my death, I want to remain united to you, if not by Communion, at least by grace and love.[39]

---

[39]   "Prayer of St. Pio of Pietrelcina after Holy Communion," Padre

More Devotions for the Art of Dying Well and a Happy Death

Litany for a Happy Death, from Bishop Richard Challoner's *The Garden of the Soul*

Composed by a Young Lady, who, at ten years of age, was converted in the Catholic Faith and died at eighteen in the odor of sanctity.

O LORD Jesus, God of goodness and Father of mercies, I approach to thee with a contrite and humble heart: to thee I recommend the last hour of my life, and the decision of my eternal doom.

When my feet, benumbed with death, shall admonish me that my mortal course is drawing to an end, Merciful Jesus, have mercy on me.

When my eyes, dim and troubled at the approach of death, shall fix themselves on thee my last and only support, Merciful Jesus, have mercy on me.

When my face, pale and livid, shall inspire the beholders with pity and dismay; when my hair, bathed in the sweat of death, and stiffening on my head, shall forebode my approaching end, Merciful Jesus, have mercy on me.

When my ears, soon to be forever shut to the discourse of men, shall be open to hear the irrevocable decree, which is to cut me off from the number of the living, Merciful Jesus, have mercy on me.

When my imagination, agitated by dreadful specters, shall be sunk in an abyss of anguish; when my soul, affrighted with the night of my iniquities and the terrors of thy judgments,

---

Pio Devotions, https://padrepiodevotions.org/stay-with-me-lord/.

shall have to fight against the angel of darkness, who will endeavor to conceal thy mercies from my eyes, and to plunge me into despair, Merciful Jesus, have mercy on me.

When the last tear, the forerunner of my dissolution, shall drop from my eyes, receive it as a sacrifice of expiation for my sins; grant that I may expire the victim of penance, and in that dreadful moment, Merciful Jesus, have mercy on me.

When my poor heart, yielding to the pressure, and exhausted by its frequent struggles against the enemies of its salvation, shall feel the pangs of death, Merciful Jesus, have mercy on me.

When my friends and relations, encircling my bed, shall shed the tear of pity over me, and invoke thy clemency in my behalf, Merciful Jesus, have mercy on me.

When I shall have lost the use of my senses, when the world shall have vanished from my sight, when my agonizing soul shall feel the sorrows of death, Merciful Jesus, have mercy on me.

When my soul, trembling on my lips, shall bid adieu to the world, and leave my body lifeless, pale and cold, receive this separation as a homage, which I willingly pay to thy Divine Majesty, and in that last moment of my mortal life, Merciful Jesus, have mercy on me.

When my last sigh shall summon my soul to burst from the embraces of the body, and to spring to thee on the wings of impatience and desire, Merciful Jesus, have mercy on me.

When at length my soul, admitted to thy presence, shall first behold the splendor of thy Majesty, reject me not, but receive me into thy bosom, where I may forever sing thy praises, and in that moment, when eternity shall begin to me, Merciful Jesus, have mercy on me.

Let us pray.

O God, who hast doomed all men to die, but hast concealed from all the hour of their death, grant that I may pass my days in the practice of holiness and justice, and that I may deserve to quit this world in the peace of a good conscience, and in the embraces of thy love, through Christ our Lord. Amen.

Prayers to St. Joseph for a Happy Death

Hail, Joseph, most holy patriarch, virginal spouse of the Virgin Mother of God and foster father of Jesus! You were worthy of seeing, hearing, embracing and saluting the infant Incarnate Word, and did enjoy the singular privilege of most sweet converse with Jesus and Mary. As it was in their arms your immaculate soul passed forth from your chaste body, be to me a powerful defender in the agony of death; and as you did surpass all in sanctity on earth and in glory among the blessed, obtain for me a holy life and a glorious immortality. Amen.

O Blessed St. Joseph, who did yield your last breath in the fond embrace of Jesus and Mary, when death shall close my career, come, holy father, with Jesus and Mary, to aid me, and obtain for me the only solace which I ask at that hour, to die under your protection. Living and dying, into your sacred hands, O Jesus, Mary and Joseph, I commend my soul.

O Glorious St. Joseph, whom I contemplate dying between Jesus and Mary, obtain for me, as well as for all those who are dear to me, the grace of leading a life like yours, so that we may die, like you, the death of the just, assisted in our last struggle by our Divine Savior and His most holy Mother. O Joseph, holy patron of a good death, I take refuge at the foot of your altar, to implore that you succor me at the moment when the sovereign Judge will call me to appear in His presence. When my eyes shall be ready to close to the light of this world, when my tongue shall be able only with difficulty to repeat the names of Jesus and Mary, come then to me — come to present my soul to God, who wished to be to you as a son, and obtain that the sentence He shall pronounce over me may make me a partaker of the glory you enjoy in heaven. Amen.

O Saint Joseph, protector of those in agony, take pity on such as at this very moment when I pray to you are engaged in their last combat. Take pity on my soul when the hour shall have come when I must wage it. Then, O my holy patron, do not abandon me; but in granting me your assistance, show that you are my good father, and grant that my Divine Savior may receive me in mercy into that abode where the elect enjoy a life that shall never end! Amen.

What to Do When Preparing for God's Judgment on Your Own

Traditionally, Lent is the penitential season when the faithful are encouraged by the Church to contemplate the four last things—death, judgement, heaven, and hell—as a spur to contrition and repentance. But emergencies, such as the COVID-19 pandemic or personal emergencies, bring into sharper focus the ever-present threat of serious illness and death and the reality of these four last things. Previous generations of Catholics took the warnings contained in Sacred Scripture and Holy Tradition seriously—that plagues and catastrophes could express God's wrath at the depravity of human sin to which we should respond with contrition and repentance. One of the blessings that comes with emergencies is that they focus our minds on the four last things, spurring us to penitential self-examination at the prospect of divine judgement that has suddenly become more real.

In 1979, the Sacred Congregation for the Doctrine of the Faith (CDF) promulgated *Certain Questions Concerning Eschatology*, which warned of doubt and unease amongst the faithful about their "destiny after death." They cautioned this was resulting in many refraining from thinking about their "destiny after death" out of fear and being adrift without a convincing theology of hope. The CDF traced this fear

to the post-conciliar controversies about fundamental doc-
trines such as the existence of the soul and eternal life that
detached the faithful from traditional truths and vocabulary;
"All this disturbs the faithful, since they no longer find the
vocabulary they are used to and their familiar ideas."

There are two traditional devotions, popular before Vatican II, that prepared and consoled the faithful for individual
judgement after death and the Last Judgement at the end
of time: devotion to Our Lord's Precious Blood and devotion to the Five Sacred Wounds of Christ. Professor Eamon
Duffy describes Christ's wounded body in these devotions
as "a hieroglyph of love": "Prayer and image have come
together by a network of associations in which the crucified
and wounded Christ features as the guarantor of the dying
Christian's hope. What began as a quasi-liturgical devotion
to the Passion becomes a deeply personal plea for redemption at the moment of death."[40]

These traditional devotions to the Precious Blood and
Sacred Wounds give us much more than a vocabulary and
ideas to understand the eschatological realities facing us.
These devotions take us deeper into our relationship with
Our Lord Jesus Christ as our Redeemer and Judge, "For all
of us must appear before the judgment seat of Christ, so that
each may receive recompense for what has been done in the
body, whether good or evil" (2 Cor 5:10).

---

[40]   Eamon Duffy, *Stripping of the Altars* (New Haven: Yale University
Press, 1992), 242.

Christ's Body Saves Us From God's Wrath

Christ's sacred body saves the righteous from the wrath of God's judgement at their sins. At death, we bring our personal history of sin into the presence of God's absolute holiness. St. Augustine describes this intersection of the foulness of our sins with the purity of God's holiness in terms of divine wrath, writing, "O man, when you appear before your Creator to be judged, you will see before you an angry God. On one side will be the sins that accuse you; on the other, the devil ready to seize you for his own. Your conscience will trouble and torment you, hell will lie open at your feet."[41]

With the tragic loss of a sense of sin, as observed by the Venerable Pope Pius XII in 1946, there has also been an almost complete and catastrophic loss of the knowledge of God's wrath, reducing divine judgement, at best, to an accounting exercise, or at worst, non-existent. Sacred Scripture and Holy Tradition make clear that eschatology has two polarities: divine wrath and divine mercy, "Whoever believes in the Son has eternal life; whoever disobeys the Son will not see life but must endure God's wrath" (Jn 3:36).

Perhaps as a consequence of naive optimism, the wrath of God is not mentioned much nowadays, even though it is a fundamental reality of God's dealings with man in the Bible. But by downplaying revelation about the wrath of God, man seeks to dethrone God as the Lord of history by only speaking of him in terms of mercy and love, misunderstood as tolerance and acceptance of man's evil and our individual sins.

---

41 St. John Bosco, *The Companion of Youth* (London: The Salesian Press, 1954), 51.

But Sacred Scripture and Holy Tradition tell us that God, as well as being merciful to the repentant, is also a God of wrath. This disturbing phrase expresses the truth that God does not passively stand aside and allow us to suffer the consequences of our sin but the more frightening reality that God actively permits us to reap the evil that we have sown through our unrepented sins as divine punishment. Sacred Scripture shows us that God's wrath is a manifestation of God's love and God's justice, because both are inextricably linked together.

St. Paul writes in his epistle to the Romans (1:18–24) that if people abandon God's laws inscribed in creation through gravely sinful acts and suppress the truth about God and man, then nations and individuals will encounter the wrath of God. He describes this as God allowing the descent of man into moral disorder, "Therefore God gave them up in the lusts of their hearts to impurity, to the degrading of their bodies among themselves, because they exchanged the truth about God for a lie and worshiped and served the creature rather than the Creator" (Rom 1:24–25).

What this means in practice is that God withdraws his graces, which are the only protection we have from sin and the devil. Once individuals and nations abandon the protection of grace, God allows them to suffer the consequences of choosing sin over him. Furthermore, one of the most frightening manifestations of God's wrath can be seen among those whose hearts are already hardened, who do not want to believe and delight in doing evil. God permits such individuals and nations to feel the total consequences of this wicked choice—hardened hearts become harder when they hear the Gospel of Our Lord Jesus Christ. St. Paul describes this in his second epistle to the Thessalonians: "For this reason God sends them a powerful delusion, leading them to believe what is false, so that all who have not believed the truth but took pleasure in unrighteousness will be condemned" (2 Thes 2:11–12).

It is important to remember that God wants to save everyone, but he does let all people who reject his offer of salvation and delight in doing evil damn themselves.

The Precious Blood of Jesus Saves Us From the Wrath of God

The righteous are saved from the wrath of God at their sins by being sacramentally immersed in the Precious Blood of Christ shed from the Precious Wounds of his Sacred Body and offered up to the Father as a perfect sacrifice on the cross: "Jesus unceasingly gazes into the face of His Father, and, with incommensurable love, He yields up His body to repair the insults offered to the Eternal Majesty: Factus obediens usque ad mortem. [He became obedient unto death.]"[42]

Abbot Vornier, commenting on St. Thomas Aquinas's insights, observes that it was the unique qualities of the Son of God's incarnate body, poured out through his blood, that constituted this perfect and irreplaceable sacrifice.[43] What are the unique qualities of the Sacred Body of Christ that make it the perfect sacrifice capable of saving us from the wrath of

---

[42]   Columba Marmion, *Christ in His Mysteries* (London: Sands & Co, 1939), 281.

[43]   Abbot Vornier, *A Key to the Doctrine of the Eucharist* (Bethesda: Zaccheus Press, 2003), 108.

God? St. Thomas Aquinas writes that it is a "Body of holiness and purity absolutely divine," quoting St. Augustine: "Is there anything so clean, with such power of cleansing away the sins of men, as that flesh, born in a womb without the least stain of carnal lust, nay, born in the womb of a Virgin? And can anything be offered up and be accepted with such grace as the flesh of our sacrifice, which has become the body of our Priest?" (ST III, q.48,a.3,ad 1.).

Father Matthias Scheeben emphasizes that the unique qualities of the Body of Christ are due to it being the human flesh assumed by the eternally begotten Son of God, and thereby sharing in the life of the Most Holy Trinity: "The human flesh of Christ corresponds to the brilliant aura of glory that suffuses Him in His divine nature, and His human blood corresponds to the river of life and love that gushes forth from His divine heart. Thus by partaking of His flesh we are illuminated by the light of eternal truth, and are transfigured and transformed by its glory; and in His blood the ocean of eternal life and divine love floods our hearts."[44]

Realizing more intensely the essential sacramental dimension of our participation in the salvific Body and Blood of Christ makes our deprivation of the sacraments due to emergencies such as COVID-19 even more painful to bear. However, God in his providence gives us, through these traditional devotions to Christ's Precious Blood and his Sacred Wounds, yet another means of benefiting from his saving graces, to add to those of Perfect Contrition and Spiritual Communion.

---

[44]   Matthias Scheeben, *The Mysteries of Christianity* (New York: Herder & Herder, 2006), 524.

Devotion to Christ's Precious Blood

Since the time of the apostles, the Precious Blood of Jesus has been drawn to the attention of the faithful for devotion, honor, and veneration as the cause of our redemption. St. Peter writes, "You know that you were ransomed from the futile ways inherited from your ancestors, not with perishable things like silver or gold, but with the precious blood of Christ, like that of a lamb without defect or blemish" (1 Pt 1:18–19).

And St. Paul writes, "Much more surely then, now that we have been justified by his blood, will we be saved through him from the wrath of God"; "In him we have redemption through his blood, the forgiveness of our trespasses, according to the riches of his grace" (Rom 5:9; Eph 1:7).

The Catechism of Pope Pius V makes it clear that the faithful should understand the "admirable fruits of the blood, shed in the Passion of our Lord":

1. The Blood of the New and Eternal Covenant gives us access to an eternal inheritance.
2. Through faith in the Blood of Christ, we have access to the righteousness of God.
3. Through the Precious Blood of Jesus, our sins are remitted.

Dr. Ludwig Ott explains that Tradition refers to the Blood of Jesus as "Precious" because, as blood of the Divine Logos, the blood of Jesus Christ is "the Precious Blood."[45] "The

---

[45]   Ludwig Ott, *Fundamentals of Catholic Dogma* (Cork: The Mercier Press, 1957), 151.

Precious Blood is therefore a part of the Sacred Humanity and hypostatically united to the Second Person of the Blessed Trinity."[46]

The soteriological significance of Jesus's blood being hypostatically united to the Son of God was explicated by Pope Clement VI in 1343, providing one of the main elements of devotion to the Precious Blood: "'With the precious blood of His very Son as of a lamb unspotted and unstained He has redeemed us' [cf.1 Pet. 1:18-19], who innocent, immolated on the altar of the Cross is known to have poured out not a little drop of blood, which however on account of union with the Word would have been sufficient for the redemption of the whole human race but copiously as a kind of flowing stream."[47]

This theme of the infinite value of the Blood of the Second Person of the Trinity has been a favorite devotional reflection of numerous saints. St. Thomas Aquinas, in his Eucharistic hymn *Adoro te devote,* writes, "Deign, O Jesus, Pelican of heaven, me, a sinner, in Thy Blood to lave, to a single drop of which is given all the world from all its sin to save."

Blessed Columba Marmion wrote, "A single drop of the Blood of Jesus, the God-man, would have sufficed to save us, for everything in Him is of infinite value."[48] Encouraging devotion to the Precious Blood, Pope St. John XXIII wrote, "Unlimited is the effectiveness of the God-Man's Blood. . . .

---

[46]   *Catholic Encyclopaedia*, s.v., "Precious Blood," https://www.newadvent.org/cathen/12372c.htm.

[47]   Pope Clement VI, *Unigenitus Dei Filius*, https://www.papalencyclicals.net/clem11/c11unige.htm.

[48]   Blessed Columba Marmion, *Christ in His Mysteries* (London: Sands & Co, 1925), 282.

Such surpassing love suggests, nay demands, that everyone reborn in the torrents of that Blood adore it with grateful love."[49] St. Teresa of Calcutta wrote, "Put your sins in the chalice for the Precious Blood to wash away. One drop is capable of washing away the sins of the world."

Devotional Prayers to the Precious Blood of Jesus

The 1926 prayer book *Devotion to the Precious Blood* outlines some of the prayers that comprise this traditional devotion.

St. Mary Magdalen de Pazzi (1566–1607) recommended, "Every time a creature offers up this Blood by which he was redeemed, he offers up a gift of infinite worth, which can be equaled by no other!"[50] She offered up the Precious Blood of Jesus fifty times a day to bring release to suffering souls in purgatory:[51]

> Eternal Father, I offer Thee the Precious Blood of Jesus, in satisfaction for my sins, and for the needs of Holy Church. Amen.

> O Eternal Father, I offer Thee, though the Immaculate Virgin Mary, the Precious Blood of Thy Son for the relief of the suffering souls in Purgatory. Amen.

The Oratorian Father Frederick Faber (1814–1863) recommended every evening, before sleep, that we "ask the Blessed Virgin Mary to offer God the Precious Blood of her Divine

---

[49]   Pope St. John XXIII, *On Promoting Devotion to the Most Precious Blood of Our Lord Jesus Christ*, https://www.papalencyclicals.net/john23/j23pb.htm.

[50]   *Devotion to the Precious Blood*, (Charlotte: TAN Books, 2012), 6.

[51]   Ibid., 14.

Son Jesus for the intention that thereby one mortal sin, which might be committed somewhere that night, might be prevented. He also expounded that if every morning this offering were renewed from day to day, we could prevent many mortal sins."[52]

> O Holy and Immaculate Virgin Mary, offer to the
> Eternal Father the Precious Blood of thy Divine Son
> for the intention that one mortal sin may be prevented
> this day (or this night). Amen.

Manifesting the truth of "Lex orandi, lex credendi," the *Litany of the Most Precious Blood* includes petitions that express how the Precious Blood of Christ saves us from the Wrath of God:[53]

> Blood of Jesus, which pacifies the wrath of the Father,
> Cleanse us, O Precious Blood!
> Blood of Jesus, which mitigates or averts
>   punishments,
> Cleanse us, O Precious Blood!
> Blood of Jesus, propitiation for our sins,
> Cleanse us, O Precious Blood!
> Blood of Jesus, cleansing bath for the sinful soul,
> Cleanse us, O Precious Blood!
> Blood of Jesus, balsam for the wounds of the soul,
> Cleanse us, O Precious Blood!

---

[52]   Ibid., 10.
[53]   Ibid., 39.

Devotion to Christ's Precious Blood During Times of Emergency

When we are deprived due to emergencies, such as the COVID-19 pandemic, from receiving in Communion the Precious Blood of Our Lord Jesus Christ, the traditional devotion to the Precious Blood of Jesus is another way of deepening our love of the Most Holy Eucharist. It enables us to join our prayers to the sacrifice of the Mass being celebrated privately by priests throughout the world.

First. Unable to have recourse to the sacrament of confession, offer up the Precious Blood of Jesus to the Father in satisfaction for your sins and the needs of the Church; so grievously impoverished by the closure of churches and the physical absence of the laity. If you are aware of any mortal sins, make an act of perfect contrition, resolve to amend your life, and go to confession as soon as possible. As you make the following prayer, unite yourself to one of the priests somewhere in the world who is at this moment offering up the Chalice of the Precious Blood of Christ:

> Eternal Father, I offer Thee the Precious Blood of Jesus, in satisfaction for my sins that I am unable to confess, and for the needs of your stricken Holy Church. Amen.

Second. With the closure of the churches and the suspension of the sacramental life of millions of the faithful, the devil seeks to tempt countless souls into the blasphemy and sacrilege of mortal sin. Every morning and night ask Our Lady to offer up the Precious Blood of her Son to the Father for the intention of stopping mortal sin in the world:

O Holy and Immaculate Virgin Mary, with so many without the protection of the sacraments, offer to the Eternal Father the Precious Blood of thy Divine Son for the intention that one mortal sin may be prevented this day (or this night). Amen.

Third. During emergencies when you cannot request Masses for the souls in purgatory, it is imperative that you frequently avail yourself of the relief offered by this devotion to the Precious Blood. If an anniversary of a loved one occurs during the closure of the churches, add their name to the following:

O Eternal Father, I offer Thee, though the Immaculate Virgin Mary, the Precious Blood of Thy Son for the relief of the suffering souls (or name of loved one) in purgatory. Amen.

Fourth. Pray the Litany of the Precious Blood before a crucifix or an image of the Holy Shroud of Turin.

Devotion to the Five Sacred Wounds

Devotion to the five sacred wounds of Christ can be traced back to St. Peter's insight into the wounds of the crucified Christ, "He himself bore our sins in his body on the cross, so that, free from sins, we might live for righteousness; by his wounds you have been healed" (1 Pt 2:24). Furthermore, the Church Fathers understood that it was Christ's intention that we approach him through his holy wounds. St. Augustine described the resurrected Christ's wounds as "the result of His power, not of some necessity."[54] St. Ambrose also

---

[54]   *The Works of Saint Augustine: A Translation for the 21st century:*

writes that Our Lord choose to keep his wounds in his glorified body: "He chose to bring to Heaven those wounds He bore for us, He refused to remove them, so that He might show God the Father the price of our freedom. The Father places Him in this state at His right hand, embracing the trophy of our salvation: such are the Witnesses the crown of scars has shown us there."

Why does Christ want us to approach him through his holy wounds? Though our sins wounded Christ, his sacred body, hypostatically united with the Second Person of the Most Holy Trinity, transforms these wounds into the means to heal the wounds of sin in ourselves.

This healing transformation is exemplified by the wound in Christ's side. From this wound flowed blood and water from his Sacred Heart, which has been traditionally understood as signifying the opening up of sanctifying grace through the sacraments. St. Augustine wrote, "Here was opened wide the door of life, from which the sacraments of the Church have flowed out, without which there is no entering unto life which is true life."[55] Commenting on Medieval devotional practices, Professor Duffy writes that the sacred wound in Christ's side "had a particular fascination and devotional power, for it gave access to his heart, and thereby became a symbol of refuge in his love."[56]

This devotion to the wounds of Christ as refuges, or hiding places, was an important expression and symbol of hope for the penitent sinner facing the struggle against the devil's

---

Letters 1-99 (New York: New City Press, 2001), 419.

[55]   Homilies on St. John the Evangelist, 120,2.

[56]   Eamon Duffy, Stripping of the Altars, 244.

onslaught of temptations as well as the prospect of being a sinner standing before God's judgement. We can hide in Christ's wounds to seek protection from the devil and we can seek merciful healing of the self-inflicted wounds of sin within the five sacred wounds.

The ancient Christological prayer the Anima Christi expresses this idea of Christ's wounds as a protective refuge against the devil.

> O good Jesus, listen to me;
> In Thy wounds I fain would hide;
> Ne'er to be parted from Thy side;
> Guard me, should the foe assail me.
> (St. John Henry Newman's translation)

St. Mechtilde's (1240–1298) famous Prayer to Five Wounds approaches each wound individually as springs of healing medicine in which to submerge sins and sinful desires, as in this extract: "I thank Thee, O Lord Jesus Christ, for the painful Wound of Thy LEFT FOOT, from which flowed the Precious Blood that washes away our sins. In it I sink and hide all the sins I have ever committed."

Julian of Norwich (1342–1416) describes the wound in Christ's side with the same sense of the infinite capacity to bring healing to man that we saw in the appreciation of a single drop of Christ's Precious Blood to wipe away all of mankind's sins: "With a kindly countenance our good Lord looked into his side, and he gazed with joy, and with his sweet regard he drew his creature's understanding into his side by the same wound; and there he revealed a fair and delectable place, large enough for all mankind that will be saved and will rest in peace and love."[57]

Thomas à Kempis (1380–1471) also saw the wounds of Christ as a consoling refuge, "Rest in Christ's Passion and live willingly in His Holy Wounds. You will gain marvelous strength and comfort in adversities."[58]

The thirteenth-century work *The Little Book of the Contemplation of Christ* also encourages devotion to the wounds of Christ with very tender imagery:

> Within the Savior's wounds there is for weak and sinful men a safe retreat. There I abide at ease, and through His wounds I pass to my Lord's Heart. All that is lacking to me, of myself, I borrow from that Heart; His mercies overflow, nor do they lack for rifts whereby they may come forth, for through His Body's wounds the secrets of His Heart are opened up, a great pledge of His kindly love is given. . . . The wounds of Jesus Christ are full of mercy, full of kindly pity, full of sweetness, full of charity. They pierced His hands and His feet and opened His side with a spear; through these clefts I may taste how gracious is the Lord my God, for gracious and gentle and exceeding merciful He is indeed to all who call upon Him in sincerity, to all who seek for Him and most of all to those who love. Plenteous redemption is given to us in the wounds of Jesus Christ our Savior, great abundance of

57   Julian of Norwich, *Showings* (New York: Paulist Press, 1978), 220.
58   Thomas à Kempis, *Imitation of Christ*, Book II/1.

sweetness, great fullness of grace, and great perfection of virtues.[59]

Having said this, the wounds of Christ also express the two polarities of eschatology: divine wrath and divine mercy. Professor Duffy writes, "It was believed that when Christ came as Judge he would display his Wounds, to the elect as pledges of his love for them, to sinners as bitter reproach — 'they shall look on him whom they have pierced.' Thus the very image which spoke of Christ's tenderness and compassion for the sinner could become a terrifying indictment of the impenitent."[60]

Making devotion to the five holy wounds of Christ part of one's life of prayer is helpful. Firstly, to gain the right disposition to receive the graces of repentance and healing that flow from his wounds in this life, and, secondly, so that they become pledges of love at our judgement after death.

Devotion to Christ's Five Holy Wounds During Emergencies

First. During emergencies, we can become cut off from our churches, our sanctuaries, from our places of refuge that protect us from the culture of death and sin that surrounds us in secular society. However, like our forefathers and mothers in the faith, we can seek refuge in the wounds of Christ. There are various traditional devotional prayers to each of the five holy wounds of Christ that will draw you deeper into these

---

[59]   *The Little Book of the Contemplation of Christ* (London: A.R. Mowbray & Co. Ltd, 1951), 55–56.

[60]   Duffy, *Stripping of the Altars*, 246.

refuges of mercy, such as St. Mechtilde's Prayer to the Five Wounds and St. Alphonsus Liguori's The Little Chaplet of the Five Wounds of Jesus Crucified (p. 71–74).

Second. Many feel called to make acts of reparation for the offence caused to Our Lord by the heresies, sacrileges, and sins abroad in the Church. Devotion to the five holy wounds of Christ is an excellent way of adopting the practice of reparation, such as Servant of God Marie Martha Chambon's The Rosary of the Holy Wounds, approved by the Sacred Congregation for the Doctrine of the Faith in 1999:

> On the large beads pray: Eternal Father, I offer Thee the Wounds of our Lord Jesus Christ. To heal the wounds of our souls.
>
> On the small beads pray: My Jesus, pardon and mercy. Through the merits of Thy Holy Wounds.

Third. Learn the *Anima Christi* by heart as a sign of your devotion to the five holy wounds of Christ and you will have at hand a ready prayer in times of crisis or reflection.

We cannot underestimate the harm being done to souls by the deprivation of the Blessed Sacrament and the sacrament of confession. The closure of the churches and the suspension of Mass during the COVID-19 pandemic is the single greatest catastrophe to devastate the Church in the whole of history of Christendom. Every enemy of the Church has sought to deprive Catholics of the Mass and reception of the Blessed Sacrament, because this is the primary objective of the devil. However, these devotions to the Precious Blood and five holy wounds of Christ are a powerful defense against this assault of the devil because they put us into touch with the Eucharistic heart of Our Lord: "The Eucharistic heart of Jesus yearns to attract our souls to itself. This heart is often humiliated, abandoned, forgotten, scorned, outraged, and yet it is the heart that loves our hearts, the silent heart that would talk to souls to teach them the value of the hidden life and the value of the ever more generous gift of self."[61]

More Devotions to Christ's Precious Blood and His Sacred Wounds

Litany in Honor of the Most Precious Blood of Jesus

For private recitation.

Lord, have mercy on us.
Christ, have mercy on us.
Lord, have mercy on us.
Christ, hear us.
Christ, graciously hear us.

God, the Father of Heaven,
Have mercy on us.
God the Son, Redeemer of the world,
Have mercy on us.
God, the Holy Ghost,
Have mercy on us.
Holy Trinity, One God,
Have mercy on us.

---

[61] Reginald Garrigou-Lagrange, *Our Saviour and His Love for Us* (Charlotte: TAN Books, 1999), 267.

Blood of Jesus, the Son of the Eternal Father,
Cleanse us, O Precious Blood!
Blood of Jesus, formed by the Holy Ghost in the
heart of the Virgin Mother,
Cleanse us, O Precious Blood!
Blood of Jesus, substantially united to the Word of
God, etc.
Blood of Jesus, of infinite majesty,
Blood of Jesus, of infinite worth,
Blood of Jesus, shed in the Circumcision,
Blood of Jesus, shed in the Agony on Mount Olivet,
Blood of Jesus, shed in the Crowning of Thorns,
Blood of Jesus, shed in the Scourging,
Blood of Jesus, shed on the Way of the Cross,
Blood of Jesus, shed at the Crucifixion,
Blood of Jesus, shed at the opening of Thy Sacred
Side,
Blood of Jesus, shed in love for mankind,
Blood of Jesus, shed in obedience to the Father,
Blood of Jesus, Sacrifice to Divine Justice,
Blood of Jesus, memorial of the bitter Passion,
Blood of Jesus, seal of the New and Eternal
Testament,
Blood of Jesus, which formed the Church, our
Mother,
Blood of Jesus, which ransomed us from the slavery
of Satan,
Blood of Jesus, which reopened Heaven for us,
Blood of Jesus, which cries more loudly than the
blood of Abel,

Blood of Jesus, which pacifies the wrath of the Father,

Blood of Jesus, which mitigates or averts punishments,

Blood of Jesus, propitiation for our sins,

Blood of Jesus, cleansing bath for the sinful soul,

Blood of Jesus, balsam for the wounds of the soul,

Blood of Jesus, source of peace and reconciliation,

Blood of Jesus, flowing in the Eucharistic Heart,

Blood of Jesus, imploring grace for us,

Blood of Jesus, flowing mystically in the Holy Sacrifice,

Blood of Jesus, inebriating drink of the children of God,

Blood of Jesus, healing drink of the sick and weak,

Blood of Jesus, refreshing drink of the banished children of Eve,

Blood of Jesus, love-potion of God-loving souls,

Blood of Jesus, celestial wine of Virgins,

Blood of Jesus, source of all consolation,

Blood of Jesus, source of love and mercy,

Blood of Jesus, source of life and holiness,

Blood of Jesus, medicine of immortality,

Blood of Jesus, reviled and despised,

Blood of Jesus, worthy of all praise,

Blood of Jesus, comfort of the Patriarchs,

Blood of Jesus, desire of the Prophets

Blood of Jesus, power and strength of the Apostles and Martyrs,

Blood of Jesus, sanctification of virgins and confessors,

Blood of Jesus, terror of evil spirits,
Blood of Jesus, salvation of those who trust in Thee,
Blood of Jesus, hope of those who die in Thee,
Blood of Jesus, consolation and refreshment of the
  Poor Souls,
Blood of Jesus, key of Heaven,
Blood of Jesus, pledge of eternal blessedness,
Blood of Jesus, delight of all the Saints,
Blood of Jesus, the Lamb without spot or blemish,

Lamb of God, Who takes away the sins of the world,
Spare us, O Lord.
Lamb of God, Who takes away the sins of the world,
Graciously hear us, O Lord.
Lamb of God, Who takes away the sins of the world,
Have mercy on us, O Lord.

You have redeemed us, O Lord, in Your Blood.
And made us a kingdom to our God.

Let us pray.

Almighty and eternal God, You have given Your only-be-
gotten Son as a Savior to the world, and Who did will to
be reconciled by His Blood, grant us, we beseech You, the
grace so to honor the Price of our Salvation, and through
its power to be protected against all the evils of the present
life, that we may enjoy the fruit thereof forever in Heaven.
Through Jesus Christ, Our Lord, Who lives and reigns with
You in the unity of the Holy Spirit, God, world without end.
Amen.

Prayer to the Holy Wounds of Jesus Christ by Saint Mechtilde

I thank Thee, O Lord Jesus Christ, for the painful Wound of Thy LEFT FOOT, from which flowed the Precious Blood that washes away our sins. In It I sink and hide all the sins I have ever committed.

Our Father.

I thank Thee, O Lord Jesus Christ, for the painful Wound of Thy RIGHT FOOT, from which the Fountain of Peace flowed to us. In Its depths I sink and bury all my desires, that they may be purified and remain unspotted by any earthly stain.

Our Father.

I thank Thee, O Lord Jesus Christ, for the painful Wound of Thy LEFT HAND, from which the Well of Grace flowed to us. In It I enclose all my spiritual and bodily ills, that in union with Thy sufferings they may become sweet to me, and by patience become a fragrant odor before God.

Our Father.

I thank Thee, O Lord Jesus Christ, for the painful Wound of Thy RIGHT HAND, from which the Medicine of the Soul was poured forth. In It I hide all my negligences and omissions which I have committed in my virtuous exercises, that they may be atoned for by Thy zealous works.

Our Father.

I thank Thee, O Lord Jesus Christ, for the healing Wound of Thy SWEETEST HEART, from which Living Water and Blood and the riches of all good flowed to us. I place myself in this Wound, and there unite all my imperfect love to Thy Divine Love, that thus it may be perfected.

Our Father.

The Little Chaplet of the Five Wounds of Jesus Crucified by St. Alphonsus Liguori

I. O my Lord Jesus Christ, I adore the wound in Your left foot. I thank You for having suffered it for me with so much sorrow and with so much love. I compassionate Your pain, and that of Your afflicted Mother. And, by the merit of this sacred wound, I pray that You grant me the pardon of my sins, of which I repent with all my heart, because they have offended Your infinite goodness. O sorrowing Mary, pray to Jesus for me.

Our Father, Hail Mary, Glory Be

> By all the wounds which You did bear
> With so much love and so much pain,
> Oh, let a sinner's prayer
> Your mercy, Lord, obtain!

II. O my Lord Jesus Christ, I adore the wound in Your right foot. I thank You for having suffered it for me with so much sorrow and with so much love. I compassionate Your pain, and that of Your afflicted Mother. And, by the merit of this sacred wound, I pray that You give me the strength not to fall into mortal sin for the future, but to persevere in Your grace until my death. O sorrowing Mary, pray to Jesus for me.

Our Father, Hail Mary, Glory Be

> By all the wounds which You did bear
> With so much love and so much pain,
> Oh, let a sinner's prayer
> Your mercy, Lord, obtain!

III. O my Lord Jesus Christ, I adore the wound in Thy left hand. I thank You for having suffered it for me with so much sorrow and with so much love. I compassionate Your pain, and that of Your afflicted Mother. And, by the merit of this sacred wound, I pray that You deliver me from Hell, which I have so often deserved, where I could never love You more. O sorrowing Mary, pray to Jesus for me.

Our Father, Hail Mary, Glory Be

> By all the wounds which Thou didst bear
> With so much love and so much pain,
> Oh, let a sinner's prayer
> Your mercy, Lord, obtain!

IV. O my Lord Jesus Christ, I adore the wound in Your right hand. I thank You for having suffered it for me with so much sorrow and with so much love. I compassionate Your pain, and that of Your most afflicted Mother. And, by the merit of this sacred wound, I pray that You give me the glory of Paradise, where I shall love You perfectly, and with all my strength. O sorrowing Mary, pray to Jesus for me.

Our Father, Hail Mary, Glory Be

> By all the wounds which You did bear
> With so much love and so much pain,
> Oh, let a sinner's prayer
> Your mercy, Lord, obtain!

V. O my Lord Jesus Christ, I adore the wound in Your side. I thank You for having willed, even after Your death, to suffer this additional injury, without pain indeed, yet with consummate love. I compassionate Your afflicted Mother, who alone felt all its pain. And, by the merit of this sacred wound, I pray You bestow upon me the gift of holy love for You, that so I may ever love You in this life, and in the other, face to face, for all eternity, in Paradise. O sorrowing Mary, pray to Jesus for me.

Our Father, Hail Mary, Glory Be

> By all the wounds which You did bear
> With so much love and so much pain,
> Oh, let a sinner's prayer
> Your mercy, Lord, obtain!

English Medieval Prayer to the Five Holy Wounds

> My crucified Jesus,
> I kiss the wounds in your Sacred Head
> With sorrow deep and true
> May every thought in my mine today
> Be an act of love for You.

> My crucified Jesus,

I kiss the wounds in your Sacred Hands
With sorrow deep and true
May every touch of my hands today
Be an act of love for You.

My crucified Jesus,
I kiss the wounds in your Sacred Feet
With sorrow deep and true
May every step I take today
Be an act of love for You.

My crucified Jesus,
I kiss the wounds in your Sacred Shoulder
With sorrow deep and true
May every cross I bear today
Be an act of love for You.

My crucified Jesus,
I kiss the wounds in your Sacred Heart
With sorrow deep and true
May every beat of my heart today
Be an act of love for you.

What to Do If a Family Member Is Dying On Their Own

From a Catholic perspective, one of the most harrowing aspects of the coronavirus pandemic is learning that many of the faithful have died alone, without the consolation of family, friends, or clergy. One of the most agonizing situations that we can face, irrespective of the virus, is knowing that a member of our family is dying, or has died, on their own, without the physical presence of those who love them at their deathbed. It can be a torment to imagine their last moments of earthly life, possibly feeling distressed, frightened, and desolate. If they have been killed in an accident or as a result of violence, we wonder if they died instantly or how long it took them to die. If they died from a sudden, catastrophic illness, or quarantined and isolated in hospital, we may imagine over and over their last moments of life. The shock of their death can cause us to suffer from post-traumatic stress disorder that makes us re-live every day the moment that we were told of their death.

The Church gives us in particular two traditional ways through which we can both be helped in our grief and assist family and friends when they physically die alone. These two devotions are to the Holy Cross and to the Sacred Heart of Jesus. These traditional devotions derive their power from our intrinsic communion with Christ through the life of grace. Before looking at these traditional devotions in more detail, it will give us hope to listen to the wisdom of saints who put how we can assist our loved ones who die physically on their own into the perspective of the supernatural life.

St. John Chrysostom writes that though distance separates us from our dying loved ones, "love unites us, and death itself cannot divide us" because through our baptism in Christ we are united in one single body, sacramentally and spiritually.[62] Our Lord was with them at their death, and because Jesus was there, we also can be there spiritually with them.

St. Pio of Pietrelcina understood that with the glorified Lord, time doesn't exist, so our prayers for loved ones at their deaths can help them at the moment of death, even if it happened in the past: "Maybe you don't know that I can pray even now for the happy death of even my great-grandfather. For the Lord, the past doesn't exist, the future doesn't exist. Everything is an eternal present. Those prayers had already been taken into account. And so, I repeat that even now I can pray for the happy death of my great-grandfather."[63]

The intimate communion between Christ and the Christian, through faith and baptism, means that we live and die in a radically new state of human existence that transcends the boundaries of space and time. This is what St. Paul means when he writes that through Baptism, the Eucharist, and all

---

62   The Divine Office, vol.III, September 13.

63   "Five Insights On Death And Dying From St. Pio Of Petrelcina," *Hour of Our Death*, October 11, 2018, https://www.hourofourdeath.org/five-insights-on-death-and-dying-from-st-pio-of-petrelcina/.

the sacraments, we live "in Christ" (2 Cor 5:17) and "in the Spirit" (1 Cor 6:17) and as members of the Body of Christ (1 Cor 12:12–28). To realize the hope within the tragedy of a family member dying physically alone, it is essential to grasp that the Body of Christ is not merely symbolic or metaphorical. We need to remember the startling reality of our new state of human existence. The Body of Christ expresses the reality that we live within the communion of the Body of Christ, (when free of mortal sin and in a state of sanctifying grace).[64] This supernatural reality of our lives can transform how we understand and respond to this tragedy. Through our union in the Body of Christ, we can be with our loved ones spiritually at the moment of their death, even if we do not learn of it until after it has happened. And, as we can be with them, we can assist them in their death.

"Who will separate us from the love of Christ? Will hardship, or distress, or persecution, or famine, or nakedness, or peril, or sword? . . . For I am convinced that neither death, nor life, nor angels, nor rulers, nor things present, nor things to come, nor powers, nor height, nor depth, nor anything else in all creation, will be able to separate us from the love of God in Christ Jesus our Lord" (Rom 8:35, 38–39).

Dying in the Lord Jesus Christ

The life of grace, opened to us by the Incarnation of the Son of God, has transformed death for the righteous Christian

---

[64]   The difference between venial and mortal sin has sometimes been neglected in modern catechisis. However, it is an important distinction since it is only by mortal sin that we cut ourselves off from the Body of Christ and reject his sanctifying grace.

from being punishment for sin to becoming the gateway to eternal life.[65] This transformation of death is a consequence of the eternal, omnipotent Son of God assuming a mortal human nature, though free from original sin, and dying on Calvary. St. Augustine explains this mysterious exchange between the life of God and the death of man:

> Who, after all, is Christ, but that Word which was in the beginning, *and the Word was with God, and the Word was God* (Jn 1:1)? This Word of God became flesh and dwelt among us. He had no power of himself to die for us: he had to take from us our mortal flesh. (Jn 1:14). You see, he would not have in himself the wherewithal to die for us, unless he had taken mortal flesh from us. That was how the immortal one was able to die, that was how he wished to bestow life on mortals; aiming later on to give us shares in himself, having first of all himself taken shares in us. I mean, we had nothing of our very own by which we could really live, and he had nothing of his very own by which he could really die. Accordingly, he struck a wonderful bargain with us, a mutual give and take; ours was what he died by; his was what we might live by.[66]

---

[65]   As Dr. Rudolph Ott puts it, "In the case of those justified by grace, death loses its penal character and becomes a mere consequence of sin." Ludwig Ott, *Fundamentals of Catholic Dogma*, trans. Patrick Lynch (Cork: The Mercier Press, 1957), 473.

[66]   *The Works of Saint Augustine: A Translation for the 21st Century.* Sermons III/6, Sermon 218C (New York: New City Press, 1993), 194.

Hilaire Belloc, the English Catholic writer and historian, saw this transformation of death for us by the eternal Son of God as the "chief miracle of the Incarnation." Belloc graphically describes death's domain as "a curtain of Iron, a gulf impassable, an impenetrable darkness, and a distance as it were limitless, infinite." The miracle brought to us by the death of the Incarnate Son of God is that "such an enormity coming upon immortal souls does not breed despair."[67] It is due to this miracle of the Incarnation that the death of our loved ones, apart from us, does not remain behind a curtain of iron, across an impassable gulf, hidden behind an impenetrable darkness, at a distance limitless, infinite. Our Lord, in his human nature, has conquered the dominion of death, changing our relationship with it. We are instead united in his body.

When the hour came for him to be glorified (Jn 12:23), Our Lord freely chose to die, unlike ordinary mortal men, showing that he had power over death and that death did not have power over him. As the *Catechism of the Council of Trent* explains, "It was the peculiar privilege of Christ the Lord to have died when He Himself decreed to die, and to have died not so much by external violence as by internal assent. Not only His death, but also its time and place, were ordained by Him."[68]

This is why Christ is depicted as a warrior entering into combat with death on his cross, and his death and resurrection properly called a triumph: "He disarmed the rulers and

---

[67]   Aidan Nichols, *Byzantine Gospel: Maximus the Confessor in Modern Scholarship* (Edinburgh: T. & T.Clark Ltd, 1993), 101.

[68]   http://www.clerus.org/bibliaclerusonline/en/dar.htm.

authorities and made a public example of them, triumph-
ing over them in it" (Col 2:15). The Anglo-Saxon poem *The
Dream of the Rood* describes Our Lord as a young warrior
entering into combat: "The young man, who was almighty
God, stripped himself, strong and unflinching. He climbed
upon the despised gallows, courageous under the scrutiny of
many, since he willed to redeem mankind."[69]

In order to see the death of Christ on the cross from a
proper Christian perspective, it is important to recollect that
Jesus Christ is Life (Jn 14:6) and that he is the complete
antithesis of death: "All things came into being through him,
and without him not one thing came into being. What has
come into being in him was life" (Jn 1:3–4). Father Aidan
Nichols, OP, rightly points out that the incarnate Son hated
death, a hatred viscerally expressed during his agony in the
garden. Our Lord hates death but accepts it to fulfil the salvific will of the Father, "The obedient love, infinite in rami-
fication, whereby the incarnate Son accepted death, though
hating it, in a free submission to the Father's will, changed
its meaning forever."[70]

Monsignor Ronald Knox, the famous English homilist
and Bible translator, preached that the miracle, that was
much more remarkable than the Resurrection was that Our
Lord "stayed dead":

---

[69]   S. A. J. Bradley, *Anglo-Saxon Poetry: An Anthology of Old English
poems in prose translation with introduction and headnotes* (London: Everyman's Library, 1982), 161.

[70]   Aidan Nichols, *The Splendour of Doctrine: The Catechism of the
Catholic Church on Christian Believing* (Edinburgh: T&T Clark,
1995), 152.

If it was an astonishing thing that our Lord should die, equally it was an astonishing thing that he should stay dead. The separation of body from soul, even in us ordinary human creatures, is not a natural state; it is an unnatural state which only takes effect because we are sinful creatures, fallen creatures, born under a curse. It's not natural for a soul to be separated from its body any more than it is natural for a fish to live out of water. And in our Lord's case there was no question of punishment for sin, no question of his having inherited the taint of fallen nature. Therefore, you would have expected that as soon as he died he would come to life again. Every second during which he stayed dead, on Good Friday and Holy Saturday and Easter Sunday morning, was a kind of miracle; a much more remarkable miracle really than his Resurrection.[71]

What is this new meaning given to our deaths by the death and resurrection of Our Lord? Death remains an evil, originating from our first parents' sin, and is contrary to God's intention, which was to endow man with "the preternatural gift of bodily immortality in Paradise."[72] Therefore, death remains our enemy, which will only be finally destroyed by Christ at the end of time (1 Cor 15:26). And as our enemy, death remains fearful and distressing on the level of nature. But on the supernatural level, death has been radically transformed for the Christian. As Father Matthias Scheeben puts it:

---

71   Ronald Knox, *The Creed in Slow Motion* (London: Sheed & Ward, 1949), 101–2.
72   Ott, *Fundamentals of Catholic Dogma*, 473.

Wonderful dispensation of divine Providence, which decreed not only to destroy death by death, but to make death itself the source of life, and ordained that we should receive supernatural life in exchange for the death of nature! In making us His children, God gives us Himself along with His entire divine glory and beatitude; and so He willed that we, too, on our part, should surrender ourselves entirely to Him in and with Christ, and should annihilate ourselves for His glory, that by this unreserved surrender of ourselves to Him we might become worthy of the unrestricted communication of Himself to us. Thus viewed, death loses the appearance of punishment, even of penance; it takes the guise of the greatest honor that man can render to God. No longer does it seem a harsh, physical necessity; nature's very weakness and frailty are to be the door to supreme glorification. Christ has drawn the sting from death, ever since the time that He Himself suffered death for us, in order to merit life for us. And ever since that time we too, in union with Him as His members, offer to God by our death the noble sacrifice that brings down upon us the fullness of divine glory.[73]

This is why it is permissible to desire death—though of course it remains a mortal sin to seek death—because it is through death that God's calls us to himself, as St. Paul expresses it, "My desire is to depart and be with Christ" (Phil 1:23). The pain of death is transformed by grace from being

---

[73]   Matthias Joseph Scheeben, *The Mysteries of Christianity* (New York: Herder & Herder, 2006), 454–55.

the pain of punishment to becoming the pains of the soul's birth into eternal life. Various saints have looked forward to their own deaths for this reason. St. Teresa of Avila wrote, "I want to see God and, in order to see him, I must die." And St. Thérèse of Lisieux said, "I am not dying; I am entering life" (CCC 1011).

The transforming power of Our Lord's radical reversal of death into life is contained in the waters of Baptism. As St. Ambrose taught the newly baptized, "Pay attention. So that in this world too the devil's snare would be broken, a rite was instituted whereby man would die, being alive, and rise again, being alive. . . . Through immersion in water the sentence is blotted out: 'You are dust, and to dust you shall return.'"[74]

Our deaths, and the deaths of our loved ones, have been united to the death of the Son of God through the waters of Baptism. If we are in a state of sanctifying grace at the moment of death, then the life of grace, begun at Baptism, comes to fruition in the beatitude of eternal life. This intrinsic union between the waters of our Baptism and the death of Our Lord on the cross is manifested by the gushing flow of water and blood from the Sacred Wound in the side and Heart of Christ, "Instead, one of the soldiers pierced his side with a spear, and at once blood and water came out" (Jn 19:34).

The power of the devotions to the Holy Cross and the Sacred Heart of Jesus to help our loved ones at the hour of death, even when we are separated by distance and time,

---

[74]   St. Ambrose, *The Navarre Bible: Saint Paul's Letter to the Romans and the Galatians* (Dublin: Four Courts Press, 2005), 91.

derive from our baptism into the saving death of the Crucified Christ.

Devotion to the Holy Cross of
Our Lord Jesus Christ

The pre-Vatican II *Rituale Romanum* instructs the priest to
bring a crucifix to the dying person as part of the Blessing
at the Hour of Death: "He gives the dying man the crucifix
to kiss and speaks to him of the confident hope of salvation
which he should have. Then he places the crucifix where
the dying person may see it and derive hope through gazing
upon it."[75]

The Litany for a Happy Death in Bishop Richard Challoner's *The Garden of the Soul* (1755) indicates that traditionally the dying held a crucifix in their hands: "When my
hands, cold and trembling, shall no longer be able to clasp
the crucifix, and, against my will, shall let it fall on my bed
of suffering, Merciful Jesus, have mercy on me."[76]

The crucifix represents to the dying many supernatural
realities around the deathbed: the need for repentance for
their sins, the punishment which Our Lord bore on the
cross, and a reminder to persevere in the hope offered by
the triumph of Christ over the devil, sin, and death. The
traditional devotion to the holy cross prepared the faithful
to enter more deeply into the significance of the crucifix at
the moment of death.

---

[75]　*The Small Ritual: Being Extracts from the Rituale Romanum in Latin & in English* (London: Burns & Oates, 1964), 127.

[76]　Richard Challoner, *The Garden of the Soul: A Manual of Devotion*
(London: Burns Oates & Washbourne Ltd, 1923), 304.

The Power of Vicarious Prayer

In a situation where a loved one has died alone without the assistance of a priest and members of their family; they are unlikely to have been able to see or hold a crucifix to bless the hour of their death. However, recalling the words of St. John Chrysostom and St. Pio of Pietrelcina—that our communion as Christians transcends distance and time—we can spiritually place, as it were, the wood of the cross in their hands through our devotions to the holy cross. The Holy Spirit gives us this ability through the power of vicarious prayer. Pope St. John Paul II describes this type of prayer as a manifestation of our lives within the communion of saints, "This is the reality of the communion of saints, the mystery of 'vicarious life'":

> Revelation also teaches that the Christian is not alone on the path of conversion. In Christ and through Christ, his life is linked by a mysterious bond to the lives of all other Christians in the supernatural union of the Mystical Body. This establishes among the faithful a marvelous exchange of spiritual gifts, in virtue of which the holiness of one benefits others in a way far exceeding the harm which the sin of one has inflicted upon others. There are people who leave in their wake a surfeit of love, of suffering borne well, of purity and truth, which involves and sustains others. This is the reality of vicariousness, upon which the entire mystery of Christ is founded. His superabundant love saves us all. Yet it is part of the grandeur of Christ's love not to leave us in the condition of passive recipients, but to

draw us into his saving work and, in particular, into his Passion.[77]

Pope St. John Paul II further explained the grace to vicariously help others by quoting St. Paul, "I am now rejoicing in my sufferings for your sake, and in my flesh I am completing what is lacking in Christ's afflictions for the sake of his body, that is, the church" (Col 1:24). Of course, Christ's sufferings are entirely sufficient to save everyone, as just one drop of his Blood is enough to save all mankind, but by joining our sufferings to those of Christ, we can assist other members of the Church. Our anguish at the death of our loved ones on their own, expressed through our devotion to the most holy cross, can vicariously assist them at the hour of their death if we pray with this intention of helping them.

The Theology of the Wood of the Cross

The Church Fathers knew that devotion to the sacred wood of the cross was particularly effective in helping us get to heaven. St. Augustine describes the necessity of the wood of the cross to help us navigate the "dangerous tempests of this world" as we seek to return to heaven:

> Now by the very nature of the voyage we are bound to endure turbulence and storms, but it's essential that at least we should stay in the boat. I mean to say, if there's danger in the boat, without the boat there's certain

---

77   Pope St. John Paul II, *Incarnationis Mysterium: Bull of Indiction of the Great Jubilee of the Year 2000*, http://www.vatican.va/jubilee_2000/docs/documents/hf_jp-ii_doc_30111998_bolla-jubilee_en.html.

destruction. However powerful the shoulders of the swimmer in the ocean, sooner or later the vastness of the sea will defeat him, and he will be swallowed up and drowned.

So it's essential we should stay in the boat, that is, that we should be carried on the wood, to be enabled to cross the sea. Now this wood, on which our feebleness is carried, is the Lord's cross, with which we are stamped and reclaimed from submersion in this world. We suffer from seasickness, but the one who will come to our aid is God.[78]

Even if there are moments when we don't know the way to heaven, if we cling to the wood of the cross, it will bear us home. "And what harm does it do a humble man if he cannot see it [heaven] from such a distance, but is coming to it nonetheless on the wood the other disdains to be carried by."[79]

To convey the power of the wood of the cross over sin and death, many saints have contrasted Christ's cross as the Tree of Life with Adam's Tree of Death—*lignum vitae crux Christi*, the Cross of Christ is the Tree of Life. St. Theodore of Studium wrote:

How precious the gift of the cross, how splendid to contemplate! In the cross there is no mingling of good

---

[78] *The Works of Saint Augustine: A Translation for the 21st Century. Sermons III/3, Sermon 75* (New York: New City Press, 1993), 304–5.

[79] Bradley G. Green, *The Gospel and the Mind: Recovering and Shaping the Intellectual Life* (Wheaton: Crossway, 2010), 94.

and evil, as in the tree of paradise: it is wholly beautiful to behold and good to taste. The fruit of this tree is not death but life, not darkness but light. This tree does not cast us out of paradise, but opens the way for our return. . . . A tree once caused our death, but now a tree brings life. Once deceived by a tree, we have now repelled the cunning serpent by a tree. What an astonishing transformation! That death should become life, that decay should become immortality, that shame should become glory![80]

St. John Chrysostom rejoiced over how the cross of Christ conquered the devil by using the "weapons of the devil" to undo his conquest of man in the Garden of Eden:

Instead of the tree of knowledge of good and evil, we have the tree of the Cross; instead of Adam's death, we have Christ's death. Do you see how the devil is vanquished by the very weapons wherewith he vanquished us? By the tree, the devil vanquished Adam; by the Cross Christ conquered the devil. That tree led to Hades, whereas the Cross led back from thence those that had been led there. And again, that tree hid the captive's nakedness, whereas the Cross revealed to all the naked Victor from on high. Adam's death condemned his descendants, whereas Christ's death raised all that had preceded Him. 'Who shall tell of the mighty acts of the Lord' (Ps. 105:2)? Out of death,

---

80   The Divine Office, Vol.II, The Office of Readings for Friday, Second Week of Easter.

to which we were subject, we became immortal. These are the accomplishments of the Cross![81]

It is for this reason that Christians, since the days of the apostles, have fostered a devotion to the holy cross of Christ—as the sure way to the glory of heaven and as having the power to reverse the injuries caused to man by Satan.

Devotional Prayers to the Holy Cross During Times of Emergency

Devotions to the cross of Christ during times of emergency will help you bring the cross of Christ spiritually to the deathbed of your loved one when you are separated by distance and time. Pray each prayer vicariously for the member of your family or a friend that you are unable to assist by your physical presence. Imagine that you have placed a crucifix in the hand of a loved one, or so that they can see it, and say the following prayers for them.

> The Cross is my sure salvation.
> The Cross I ever adore.
> The Cross of my Lord is with me.
> The Cross is my refuge. (St. Thomas Aquinas)

We adore You, O Christ, and we bless You, because by Your Holy Cross You have redeemed the world. (St. Alphonsus Liguori)

---

[81]   John Sanidopoulos, "St. John Chrysostom's Homily On the Cemetery and the Cross (Excerpts)," May 3, 2011, https://www. johnsanidopoulos.com/2011/05/st-john-chrysostoms-homily-on-cemetery.html.

Come, O beloved, let us cover ourselves below the wings of the precious and life-giving Cross. For the four ends of the Cross signifies that He Who was crucified upon it is God over all places and has received all from the ends of the earth. Christ God was lifted up upon it, that He might dissolve the demons that infested the air, and made our passage to heaven unhindered, as our Savior Himself told us: "When I am lifted from the earth, I will draw all men towards me" (John 12:32). (St. John Chrysostom)

> By the cross death is destroyed,
> and by the cross salvation shines;
> by the cross the gates of hell are burst,
> and by the cross the gates of paradise are opened.
> The cross is the destroyer of hell. (St. Melito of
> Sardis)

Oh Lord Almighty! You have suffered death at the cross for our sins. Oh, Holy Cross of Jesus! be my true light. Oh, Holy Cross of Jesus! fill my soul with good thoughts. Oh, Holy Cross! help me in my salvation. Oh, Holy Cross! safeguard me against unholy thoughts and worldly dangers that I may worship the Holy Cross of Jesus of Nazareth crucified. Have pity on me. Oh, Holy Cross of Jesus! be my hope. Oh, Holy Cross have mercy on me forever and ever. Amen.

Prayer Before a Crucifix

Behold, O kind and most sweet Jesus,
I cast myself upon my knees in Thy sight,
and with the most fervent desire of my soul
I pray and beseech Thee

to impress upon my heart
lively sentiments of faith,
hope and charity,
with true repentance for my sins
and a most firm desire of amendment:
whilst with deep affection and grief of soul
I consider within myself
and mentally contemplate Thy five most precious
    Wounds,
having before mine eyes that which David, the
    prophet,
long ago spoke in Thine own person concerning
    Thee,
my Jesus: "They have pierced My hands and My feet,
they have numbered all My bones."

A plenary indulgence, under the usual conditions, is attached to the recitation of this prayer on the Fridays in Lent and throughout Passiontide (last two weeks of Lent). At other times, a partial indulgence can be obtained. (See the appendix on Indulgences.)

There are more devotional prayers to the holy cross at the end of this chapter, including the *Litany of the Holy Cross*.

Pray for the Intercession of the Saints Associated With the Cross of Christ

In addition to praying these devotional prayers, ask for the help of saints for the loved one who is dying physically on their own, and for yourself and your family. "It is good and useful suppliantly to invoke them [saints], and to have recourse to their prayers, aid, and help for obtaining benefits from God, through His Son Jesus Christ our Lord" (Council of Trent). As well as the patron saint of your loved one, ask for the intercession of saints associated with the cross of Christ, such as Our Lady, St. John the Apostle, and St. Mary Magdalene, who all stood at the foot of the cross as Our Lord died.

Also, saints who bore the wounds of Christ as stigmata should be approached for help, including, for example, St. Francis of Assisi, St. Catherine of Siena, St. Gemma Galgani, and St. Pio of Pietrelcina. As St. Gemma Galgani lay dying on Good Friday, 1903, she said to the sister who was nursing her, "Don't leave me until I'm nailed on the cross. I have to be crucified with Jesus. Jesus told me that his children have to be crucified with him." Then she extended her arms and remained in the posture of Jesus dying on the cross for three hours.[82]

Devotions to the Sacred Heart of Jesus

St. Margaret Mary Alacoque's devotions to the Sacred Heart and St. Faustina Kowalska's Divine Mercy devotion, with its sacred painting of blue and red rays radiating from Jesus's chest, take us deep into the heart of Christ's Paschal Mystery. Cardinal Ratzinger observes that "devotion to the Sacred Heart is in touch with a central biblical reality — that it is an Easter spirituality."[83] Both devotions are charged with

---

[82]   "St Gemma Galgani –The lover of Jesus," *Mystics of the Church*, https://www.mysticsofthechurch.com/2009/12/st-gemma-galgani-lover-of-jesus.html.

[83]   Joseph Cardinal Ratzinger, *Behold the Pierced One: An Approach to*

the life-giving waters of Christ, "The water that I will give will become in them a spring of water gushing up to eternal life" (Jn 4:14). Cardinal Ratzinger advises that in order to get a true understanding of devotions to the Sacred Heart of Jesus, we must view them through the Johannine revelation of Jesus as the source of "living water," especially these two passages from John's Gospel: "One of the soldiers pierced his side with a spear, and at once blood and water came out" (Jn 19:34); "'Let anyone who is thirsty come to me, and let the one who believes in me drink. As the scripture has said, 'Out of the believer's heart shall flow rivers of living water.' Now he said this about the Spirit, which believers in him were to receive; for as yet there was no Spirit, because Jesus was not yet glorified" (Jn 7:37–39).

Through devotion to the Sacred Heart during the emergency of a loved one dying physically on their own, we can immerse them and ourselves into the river of eternal life that constantly flows from the sacred heart of Jesus.

The Theology of the Sacred Heart

Watching cinematic reenactments of the piercing of Our Lord's dead body with a spear during his crucifixion can give the impression that he was passive and powerless to the actions of the Roman soldiers. However, it is important to keep in mind that though the Son of God in his human nature was a vulnerable victim, in his omnipotent divine nature he allowed the spear to be thrust into his side. Church Fathers and saints down the ages have been fascinated with

---

Spiritual Christology (San Francisco: Ignatius Press, 1984), 49.

why the Son of God permitted the piercing of his Sacred Heart. St. Augustine sees the wounding of the side as Christ opening the gate of life:

> A suggestive word was made use of by the evangelist, in not saying pierced, or wounded His side, or anything else, but "opened;" that thereby, in a sense, the gate of life might be thrown open, from whence have flowed forth the sacraments of the Church, without which there is no entrance to the life which is the true life. That blood was shed for the remission of sins; that water it is that makes up the health-giving cup and supplies at once the laver of baptism and water for drinking. . . . O death, whereby the dead are raised anew to life! What can be purer than such blood? What more health-giving than such a wound?[84]

St. Bernard understands that Christ allowed his Sacred Heart to be opened so that we might rest secure in the protection of God's love:

> Your sacred side was pierced only *to open for us a way into your Heart* and this Heart itself was laid open only that we might be able *to dwell therein* in perfect freedom, secure from all that could disturb our rest. . . . This adorable Heart was wounded in order that by this visible wound we might come to know of the invisible wound that love had made. Ah, how could Jesus show His ardent love more plainly than by willing that not

---

[84] St. Augustine, Tractate 120 (John 19:31-20:9), https://www. newadvent.org/fathers/1701120.htm.

only His Body, but moreover His very Heart should be pierced by the spear? . . . Who can help loving a Heart thus wounded? Who can remain insensible to its love?[85]

The opening up of Our Lord's heart on the cross, from which gushes forth living streams of baptismal water and Eucharistic blood, is a theophany of the heart of the Most Holy Trinity. As Cardinal Joseph Ratzinger writes, "In the pierced heart of the Crucified, God's own heart is opened up; here we see who God is and what he is like. Heaven is no longer locked up. God has stepped out of his hiddenness. That is why St. John sums up both the meaning of the Cross and the nature of the new worship of God in the mysterious promise made through the prophet Zechariah (cf. 12:10). 'They shall look on him whom they have pierced' (Jn 19:37)."[86]

Devotions to the Sacred Heart of Christ During Times of Emergency

The wound in the Sacred Heart of Our Lord Jesus Christ is a gateway to a refuge, a sanctuary, of divine love that offers protection from the storms of evil that assail us during our lives. Our Lord also helped St. Margaret Mary Alacoque and St. Faustina Kowalska understand that his Sacred Heart is especially a place of refuge during the final hour of our death.

---

[85]   Joseph De Galliffet, *The Adorable Heart of Jesus* (London: The Catholic Truth Society, 1887), 218.

[86]   Joseph Cardinal Ratzinger, *The Spirit of the Liturgy* (San Francisco: Ignatius Press, 2000), 48.

St. Margaret Mary Alacoque

In his apparition to St. Margaret Mary Alacoque, Our Lord made promises to those who had a devotion to his Sacred Heart, one of which was "I will be their strength during life and above all during death": "In the excess of the mercy of my Heart, I promise you that my all powerful love will grant to all those who will receive Communion on the First Fridays, for nine consecutive months, the grace of final repentance: they will not die in my displeasure, nor without receiving the sacraments; and my Heart will be their secure refuge in that last hour."

St. Margaret Mary went on to compose a Consecration to the Most Sacred Heart of Jesus that included the expression of confidence in the Sacred Heart as a refuge at the hour of death: "I therefore take You, O Sacred Heart, to be the only object of my love, the guardian of my life, my assurance of salvation, the remedy of my weakness and inconstancy, the atonement for all the faults of my life and my sure refuge at the hour of death."

During the death of your loved one, pray that they receive the grace to experience Our Lord's Sacred Heart as a place of refuge within which they feel surrounded by the protection of his love.

St. Faustina Kowalska

At the heart of the devotion of Divine Mercy is Our Lord's passion, with the sacred image of Jesus showing water and blood radiating from the holy wound in his Sacred Heart. Our Lord promised St. Faustina that we could pray the

Divine Mercy Chaplet vicariously for the dying and that they would benefit from the indulgence. "At the hour of their death, I defend as My own glory every soul that will say this chaplet; or when others say it for a dying person, the indulgence is the same. When this chaplet is said by the bedside of a dying person, . . . unfathomable mercy envelops the soul, and the very depths of My tender mercy are moved" (Diary, 811).

St. Faustina was also graced by Our Lord with a special communion with the dying and recounts in her diary that dying souls came to her for assistance and she accompanied them praying the Rosary or the Divine Mercy Chaplet. When St. Faustina had the sense that they had died, she concluded with the *De Profundis* (Psalm 130). She writes:

> Especially now, while I am in the hospital, I experience an inner communion with the dying who ask me for prayer when their agony begins. God has given me a wondrous contact with the dying! . . . O God of fathomless mercy, who allow me to give relief and help to the dying by my unworthy prayer, be blessed as many thousand times as there are stars in the sky and drops of water in all the oceans! Let Your mercy resound throughout the orb of the earth, and let it rise to the foot of Your throne, giving praise to the greatest of Your attributes; that is, Your incomprehensible mercy.
> (*Diary*, 835)

St. Faustina's care of the dying during her life makes her an ideal intercessor for your loved ones during the hour of their death.

St. Francis de Sales

Devotion to the Sacred Heart can also enable us to be in communion with our loved ones when separated by distance and time, especially if they have a devotion to the Sacred Heart themselves. St. Francis de Sales understood the Sacred Heart to be a sanctuary where those who are separated can enter into spiritual closeness: "I do not know where you will be this Lent according to the body, but according to the spirit I hope you will always be . . . in the pierced side of our dear Savior. I hope to try to be often with you there. God in His sovereign goodness grant us both the grace!"[87]

Pray before a sacred image of Our Lord's Sacred Heart for the grace to be spiritually close to your loved one as they die.

The hour of death is the climax of our life's striving for Christian perfection, through the grace of God. It is the final battle with Satan to save our soul. This is why the assistance of priests and our family at the deathbed is so important. In emergencies where members of your family face dying physically on their own, you are like the women disciples who accompanied Our Lord to his crucifixion: "Many women were also there, looking on from a distance; they had followed Jesus from Galilee and had provided for him. Among them were Mary Magdalene, and Mary the mother of James and Joseph, and the mother of the sons of Zebedee" (Mt 27:55–57).

St. Mary Magdalene and the other women were as close to Jesus as family, providing for his needs, and they continued to support him from a distance as best they could as he

---

[87]   Joseph de Galliffet, *The Adorable Heart of Jesus*, 220.

died alone on the cross. Through our prayers, and devotions such as those to the most holy cross and the Sacred Heart of Jesus, we spiritually stand around our loved ones as they die, with the angels and saints, supporting them in their final struggle with evil. We pray that our loved ones are triumphant over death through the cross of Christ and that they enter into the Sacred Heart of Divine Mercy, "If we have died with him, we will also live with him; if we endure, we will also reign with him" (2 Tm 2:12).

More Devotions to the Holy Cross and the Sacred Heart of Jesus
Litany of the Holy Cross

For Private Use Only.

Lord, have mercy. *Lord, have mercy.*
Christ, have mercy. *Christ, have mercy.*
Lord, have mercy. *Lord, have mercy.*
Christ, hear us. *Christ, graciously hear us.*

God the Father of heaven, *have mercy on us.*
God the Son, Redeemer of the world, *have mercy on us.*
God the Holy Spirit, our Advocate, *have mercy on us.*
Holy Trinity, one God, *have mercy on us.*

Holy Cross whereon the Lamb of God was offered, *save us, O Holy Cross.*
Hope of Christians, *save us, O Holy Cross.*

Pledge of the resurrection of the dead, *save us, O Holy Cross.*

Shelter of persecuted innocence, *save us, O Holy Cross.*

Guide of the blind, *save us, O Holy Cross.*

Way of those who have gone astray, *save us, O Holy Cross.*

Staff of the lame, *save us, O Holy Cross.*

Consolation of the poor, *save us, O Holy Cross.*

Restraint of the powerful, *save us, O Holy Cross.*

Destruction of the proud, *save us, O Holy Cross.*

Refuge of sinners, *save us, O Holy Cross.*

Trophy of victory over Hell, *save us, O Holy Cross.*

Terror of demons, *save us, O Holy Cross.*

Mistress of youth, *save us, O Holy Cross.*

Succor of the distressed, *save us, O Holy Cross.*

Hope of the hopeless, *save us, O Holy Cross.*

Star of the mariner, *save us, O Holy Cross.*

Harbor of the wrecked, *save us, O Holy Cross.*

Rampart of the besieged, *save us, O Holy Cross.*

Father of orphans, *save us, O Holy Cross.*

Defense of widows, *save us, O Holy Cross.*

Counsel of the just, *save us, O Holy Cross.*

Judge of the wicked, *save us, O Holy Cross.*

Rest of the afflicted, *save us, O Holy Cross.*

Safeguard of childhood, *save us, O Holy Cross.*

Strength of manhood, *save us, O Holy Cross.*

Last hope of the aged, *save us, O Holy Cross.*

Light of those who sit in darkness,

Splendor of kings, *save us, O Holy Cross.*

Civilizer of the world, *save us, O Holy Cross.*
Shield impenetrable, *save us, O Holy Cross.*
Wisdom of the foolish, *save us, O Holy Cross.*
Liberty of slaves, *save us, O Holy Cross.*

Knowledge of the ignorant, *save us, O Holy Cross.*
Sure rule of life, *save us, O Holy Cross.*
Heralded by prophets, *save us, O Holy Cross.*
Preached by apostles, *save us, O Holy Cross.*
Glory of martyrs, *save us, O Holy Cross.*
Study of hermits, *save us, O Holy Cross.*
Chastity of virgins, *save us, O Holy Cross.*
Joy of priests, *save us, O Holy Cross.*
Foundation of the Church, *save us, O Holy Cross.*
Salvation of the world, *save us, O Holy Cross.*
Destruction of idolatry, *save us, O Holy Cross.*
Stumbling block to unbelievers, *save us, O Holy Cross.*
Condemnation of the ungodly, *save us, O Holy Cross.*
Support of the weak, *save us, O Holy Cross.*
Medicine of the sick, *save us, O Holy Cross.*
Health of the lepers, *save us, O Holy Cross.*
Strength of the lame, *save us, O Holy Cross.*
Bread of the hungry, *save us, O Holy Cross.*
Fountain of those who thirst, *save us, O Holy Cross.*
Clothing of the naked, *save us, O Holy Cross.*

Lamb of God, Who takes away the sins of the world,
Spare us, O Lord.
Lamb of God, Who takes away the sins of the world,
Hear us, O Lord.
Lamb of God, Who takes away the sins of the world,
Have mercy on us.

Christ, hear us. Christ, graciously hear us.
Lord, have mercy. Lord, have mercy.
Christ, have mercy. Christ, have mercy.
Lord, have mercy. Lord, have mercy.
V. We adore You, O Christ, and we bless You,
R. Because by Your Holy Cross you have redeemed
the world.

Behold the Cross of the Lord! Be gone, you evil
powers!
The Lion of the tribe of Judah, the Root of David,
has conquered! Alleluia!

Let Us Pray.

O God, for the redemption of the world You were pleased
to be born in a stable and to die upon a cross; O Lord Jesus
Christ, by Your holy sufferings, which we, Your unworthy
servants, call to mind: by Your Holy Cross, and by Your
death, deliver us from the pains of Hell, and graciously grant
that You will conduct us where You conducted the good thief
who was crucified with You, who live and reign eternally in
Heaven. R. Amen.

Sweet the wood, sweet the nails, sweet the Burden
which You bear,
for You alone, O Holy Cross, were worthy to bear the
King and Lord of heaven.
R. Amen.[88]

---

[88]   Paul Thigpen, *Manual for Spiritual Warfare* (Charlotte: TAN
Books, 2014) 290–94.

Prayer for the Faithful in Their Agony

O Most merciful Jesus, Lover of souls: I pray that You, by the agony of Your most Sacred Heart, and by the sorrows of Your Immaculate Mother, cleanse in Your own Blood the sinners of the whole world who are now in their agony and to die today. *Amen.*

Heart of Jesus, once in agony, *Pity the dying.*[89]

Jesus, I live for You;
Jesus, I die for You;
Jesus, I am Yours in life and death.

St. Faustina Kowalska's Divine Mercy Chaplet

You expired, Jesus, but the source of life gushed forth for souls, and the ocean of mercy opened up for the whole world. O Fount of Life, unfathomable Divine Mercy, envelop the whole world and empty Yourself out upon us.

O Blood and Water, which gushed forth from the Heart of Jesus as a fount of mercy for us, I trust in You! (Repeat three times.)

Our Father, Hail Mary, Apostles Creed

On the Large Beads:

Eternal Father, I offer you the Body and Blood, Soul and Divinity of Your Dearly Beloved Son, Our Lord, Jesus

---

[89]   English Bishops, *The Manual of Prayers For Congregational and Home Use* (London: Burns Oates and Washbourne Ltd, 1922), 213.

Christ, in atonement for our sins and those of the whole world.

On the Small Beads:

For the sake of His sorrowful Passion, have mercy on us and on the whole world.

After praying five decades, pray the closing prayer:

Holy God, Holy Mighty One, Holy Immortal One, have mercy on us and on the whole world. (Repeat three times.)

Optional closing prayer:

Eternal God, in whom mercy is endless and the treasury of compassion inexhaustible, look kindly upon us and increase Your mercy in us, that in difficult moments we might not despair nor become despondent, but with great confidence submit ourselves to Your holy will, which is Love and Mercy itself.

St. Margaret Mary Alacoque's Efficacious Novena to the Sacred Heart of Jesus

St. Pio of Pietrelcina (Padre Pio) prayed this novena every day in response to requests for prayer.

I.

O my Jesus, you have said: "Truly I say to you, ask and you will receive, seek and you will find, knock and it will be opened to you." Behold I knock, I seek and ask for the grace of (here name your request).

Our Father, Hail Mary, Glory Be to the Father, Sacred Heart of Jesus, I place all my trust in you.

II.

O my Jesus, you have said: "Truly I say to you, if you ask anything of the Father in my name, he will give it to you." Behold, in your name, I ask the Father for the grace of (here name your request).

Our Father, Hail Mary, Glory Be to the Father, Sacred Heart of Jesus, I place all my trust in you.

III.

O my Jesus, you have said: "Truly I say to you, heaven and earth will pass away but my words will not pass away." Encouraged by your infallible words I now ask for the grace of (here name your request).

Our Father, Hail Mary, Glory Be to the Father, Sacred Heart of Jesus, I place all my trust in you.

O Sacred Heart of Jesus, for whom it is impossible not to have compassion on the afflicted, have pity on us miserable sinners and grant us the grace which we ask of you, through the Sorrowful and Immaculate Heart of Mary, your tender Mother and ours.

Pray the *Hail, Holy Queen* and add St. Joseph, foster father of Jesus, pray for us.

What to Do if Grieving Without the Assistance of a Priest

Grieving after the traumatic death of a loved one can be like waking up into a nightmare world in which we feel everything that was certain and reliable has become unpredictable and unstable. We can even feel like we've become a different person—pain-racked, desperate, tempted to despair. Grief has a life of its own that hijacks your thoughts and feelings without any warning as you try to go about your normal life. Anything can trigger it—a chance comment, a piece of music, a TV program, a memory, a passage of Sacred Scripture, being hugged.

Close relationships can become strained and difficult with other members of the family because people respond differently to grief, especially as men and women cope with it in very different ways. Though this is a generalization, and of course there will be exceptions, men tend to cope with grief by throwing themselves into work and activity in an attempt to escape the pain, while women cope through talking and physical intimacy. Problems happen in marriages when these different ways of coping with grief lead to husbands and wives feeling isolated and lonely at the time when they most need understanding and love.

The pain of grief can be so intense, and at times unbearable, that it is not uncommon for people to be tempted to commit suicide. This danger is heightened if those grieving resort to alcohol or drugs to numb the pain. The Church's categorical teaching of God's absolute prohibition against suicide can be a strong anchor during such storms of grief.

Father Benedict Groeschel writes that "the death of those who are dear to us, of those on whom we have relied, is life's worst pain" and can lead "believers to waver a bit in their firmness of faith and makes many of the weak stumble."[90]

For all these reasons, the assistance of clergy following the death of a loved one is so important, especially if it was traumatic and you were unable to be with them when they died. The COVID-19 pandemic, with the closure of churches and the restriction of priestly ministry, has meant that many of the faithful have had to cope with grief on their own. But the fact of the matter is, even with the assistance of clergy, coping with grief caused by the traumatic death of a loved one is extremely challenging and difficult.

There are two traditional devotions that can help you weather the storms of grief: the *imitatio Christi* and the *imitatio Mariae*, the Imitation of Christ and the Imitation of Mary. As one would expect, the *imitatio Mariae* is orientated to lead to a deeper, more profound *imitatio Christi,* as St. Louis Grignion de Montfort understood, *Ad Jesum Per Mariam,* "To Jesus through Mary."

A sure means of finding your way through the intense disorientation and extreme suffering of grief is by asking for

---

90   Benedict J. Groeschel, *Arise from Darkness: When Life Doesn't Make Sense* (San Francisco: Ignatius Press, 1995), 105.

the grace to be more and more like Our Lord Jesus Christ and the Blessed Virgin Mary. If this seems too overwhelming a prospect for you during this moment of grief, just spending more time in the company of Our Lord and his mother through these devotions will be a consolation and an encouragement and a source of great graces such as the gifts of fortitude and hope.

Only the Mystery of Jesus Sheds Light on the Mystery of Man

Death confronts us with the mystery of our own existence, raising fundamental questions about the meaning and purpose of our life: What's the point of it all? Why did God allow my loved one to die? Is death the last word? Why does God allow us to suffer? Where is God in all this suffering? Why didn't God answer my prayers? Church Fathers and saints down the ages have taught, by words and deeds, that only Jesus Christ, the Incarnate Son of God, can answer these mysterious questions about life and death, which especially torment the grieving. Pope St. John Paul II's favorite passage from the Second Vatican Council was about these mysterious questions of man finding their answer in Jesus:

> The truth is that only in the mystery of the incarnate Word does the mystery of man take on light. For Adam, the first man, was a figure of Him Who was to come, namely Christ the Lord. Christ, the final Adam, by the revelation of the mystery of the Father and His love, fully reveals man to man himself and makes his supreme calling clear. It is not surprising, then, that in

Him all the aforementioned truths find their root and attain their crown. He Who is "the image of the invisible God" (Col. 1:15), is Himself the perfect man. . . . By suffering for us He not only provided us with an example for our imitation, He blazed a trail, and if we follow it, life and death are made holy and take on a new meaning.[91]

Through his incarnation and Paschal Mystery—his life, death, resurrection and glorification—Christ has redeemed our life and death from the dominion of evil. If, through the help of his grace, we imitate Our Lord in our suffering and grief, we will find that he sanctifies life and death for us, giving both a radical new meaning.

Faith enables us to participate in Christ's mysteries through every dimension of our existence—intellectually, emotionally, physically, and spiritually. Christ's mysteries are not dead history but living realities that we can share in here and now through faith and the sacraments of the Church. Our participation in his mysteries is the whole purpose of the Incarnation, so that we would, through the graciousness of God, come to share the divine nature (2 Pt 1:4).

Christ gives us the grace to be able to not only bear but grow through our suffering and grief by enabling us to share in his mysteries in three ways:

Christ lived his mysteries for us. Everything Christ said and did was an expression of his love for us. He lived all his mysteries so that each one of us will attain our destiny

---

[91]   *Gaudium et Spes*, no. 22, http://www.vatican.va/archive/hist_ councils/ii_vatican_council/documents/vat-ii_const_19651207_ gaudium-et-spes_en.html.

of sharing the life of God. As Blessed Columba Marmion explains:

> It was veritably for us that He came down from Heaven, in order to redeem us and save us from death: *Propter nos homines et propter nostram salute;*[92] it was to give us life: *Ego veni ut vitam habeant, et abundantius habeant.*[93] He had no need to satisfy and to merit for Himself, for He is the very Son of God, equal to the Father, at Whose right hand He is seated in the heights of Heaven; but it was for us that He bore everything. For us He became Incarnate, was born at Bethlehem, and lived in the obscurity of a life of toil; for us He preached and worked miracles, died and rose again; for us He ascended into Heaven and sent the Holy Spirit; He still remains in the Eucharist for us, for love of us.[94]

Christ lived with the grief of the death of his stepfather Joseph. When he heard of the death of John the Baptist, he withdrew to a deserted place by himself (Mt 14:13). He wept at the death of his friend Lazarus (Jn 11:35), and he was filled with compassion for the widow of Nain whose son had died (Lk 7:13). He lives through the turmoil of human grief so that he can share with us in compassionate understanding our sufferings and grief.

---

[92] "For us men and for our salvation."

[93] "I came that they may have life, and have it abundantly" (Jn 10:10).

[94] Dom Columba Marmion, *Christ in His Mysteries* (London: Sands & Co, 1939), 11.

Christ lived his mysteries to be our model. Christ shows us how to live a life that fulfills and realizes our capacity to enter into a relationship with God. Each of his mysteries is a revelation of his virtues, so that sharing in them and imitating them we may become more like him. As Blessed Columba Marmion writes:

> He has come to be our Model. It is not only to announce salvation to us and to work out in principle our redemption that the Word becomes Incarnate; it is also to be the ideal of our souls. Christ Jesus is God living in our midst; — God appearing amongst us, rendered visible and tangible, and showing us by His life as well as by His words the way of holiness. We have no need to seek elsewhere than in Him for the model of our perfection. Each of His mysteries is a revelation of His virtues. . . . Jesus, through His mysteries, has, so to speak, marked out all the stages which, in the supernatural life, we must follow after Him; or rather, He Himself draws the faithful soul with Him in the way that He runs as a giant: *Exsultavit ut gigas ad currendam viam.*[95] "I created souls in My image and likeness," said our Lord to St. Catherine of Siena; "even more, in taking human nature, I made Myself like one of you. Consequently, I do not cease working to make souls like to Me, as far as they are capable of it, and I endeavor to renew in them, when they are tending towards heaven, all that took place in My Body."[96]

---

[95]   "Like a strong man runs its course with joy" (Ps 19:5).
[96]   Dom Columba Marmion, *Christ in His Mysteries*, 12–13.

Taking Christ as our model, we may weep and go to a deserted place while still sharing in complete confidence his promise, "I am the resurrection and the life. Those who believe in me, even though they die, will live" (Jn 11:25).

Christ Enables Us to Unite Our Lives With His Life Through His Mysteries

Through the faith handed to us by the apostles and expressed through the sacraments, our upholding of doctrine, our prayers, and our moral life, our lives are united, through grace, to the life of Christ. Each one of us is called to make real in our own lives these words of St. Paul, "I have been crucified with Christ; and it is no longer I who live, but it is Christ who lives in me. And the life I now live in the flesh I live by faith in the Son of God, who loved me and gave himself for me" (Gal 2:19–20). It is through our union to Christ that we can bear the pain of grief, experience its weight without it crushing us, and gradually transform it into an act of love.

To those in a state of grace, the mysteries of Our Lord Jesus Christ are not distant or extraneous, imposed on us from outside, but the answer to be found deep within ourselves, made in the image of God, restored by the sanctifying grace of Baptism. As St. Augustine puts it, "Lo, you were within, but I outside, seeking there for you."[97] Within the intimacy of our hearts, Christ comforts us in our grief, shares with us his own transforming love, and conforms us to himself.

---

[97]   *The Works of Saint Augustine: A Translation for the 21st Century. The Confessions* (New York: New City Press, 1997), 262.

Imitating the New Adam

We are able to find Jesus within ourselves because he is the New Adam, who has "penetrated in a unique unrepeatable way into the mystery of man and entered his 'heart.'"[98] It is important to realize that the answers to the anguished questions of our grief found in the New Adam are not theoretical, philosophical, or ideological but are the revelation of the Person of Jesus Christ: "Jesus lived an authentic human life, and we know that the difficulties he encountered were such as to make him always and forever close to all who have to endure trials and sufferings in their own lives."[99]

The Son of God's assumption of human nature is an event that effects every human being. Cardinal Karol Wojtyla explains that whether or not individuals accept the re-birth of mankind in the New Adam in the redemptive death and resurrection of Jesus, "at that moment man's existence acquired a new dimension, very simply expressed by St. Paul as 'in Christ.'" "Man exists 'in Christ', and he had so existed from the beginning in God's eternal plan; but it is by virtue of Christ's death and resurrection that this 'existence in Christ' became historical fact, with roots in time and space."[100]

What does it mean to exist "in Christ," to be the "new man" brought into being through faith and Baptism, "so we too might walk in newness of life" (Rom 6:4)? It means living day to day with the awareness that through sanctifying

---

[98] Pope St. John Paul II, *Redemptor Hominis*, http://www.vatican.va/content/john-paul-ii/en/encyclicals/documents/hf_jp-ii_enc_04031979_redemptor-hominis.html.

[99] Karol Wojtyla, *Sign of Contradiction* (Slough: St Paul Publication, 1979), 102.

[100] Ibid., 91.

grace, the Most Holy Trinity dwells in our hearts and that consequently we view this worldly life from the perspective of our true homeland, heaven.

St. Paul writes that through our Baptism into Christ's death and resurrection and our reception of the Holy Spirit, we no longer belong to the first Adam's "world of dust," now we belong to the second Adam's heavenly realm: "The first man was from the earth, a man of dust; the second man is from heaven. As was the man of dust, so are those who are of the dust; and as is the man of heaven, so are those who are of heaven. Just as we have borne the image of the man of dust, we will also bear the image of the man of heaven" (1 Cor 15:47–49).

Heaven is our homeland because Christ, in his human nature, has ascended to heaven and is seated at the right hand of the Father in glory, which should reorientate the focus of our lives away from the sinful illusions of this world and towards the glorious truths of heaven: "So, if you have been raised with Christ, seek the things that are above, where Christ is, seated at the right hand of God. Set your minds on things that are above, not on things that are on earth, for you have died, and your life is hidden with Christ in God" (Col 3:1–3).

Father Albert Gelin, SS, sees this passage from Colossians as the Christian program we must follow to make present in ourselves the man from heaven, the New Adam, through the grace of God and with the assistance of the Holy Spirit.[101]

---

[101]   Albert Gelin, *The Concept of Man in the Bible* (London: Geoffrey Chapman, 1968), 160.

To see everything in your life from the perspective of heaven, even your grief, is to live as Our Lord commanded: "Do not store up for yourselves treasures on earth, where moth and rust consume and where thieves break in and steal; but store up for yourselves treasures in heaven, where neither moth nor rust consumes and where thieves do not break in and steal. For where your treasure is, there your heart will be also" (Mt 6:19–21).

Our grief and suffering may not be diminished but reframed in the light of heaven, our questions about meaning and purpose no longer overwhelm us. Sharing in Christ, we are given strength and hope.

The Blessed Virgin Mary Uniquely Helps Us Imitate the New Adam

As the mother of the incarnate Son of God, the Blessed Virgin Mary has a unique role in helping us realize in ourselves her Son, the New Adam. This unique role derives from the fact that the Son of God assumed a human nature through the flesh of the Blessed Virgin Mary. Mary contributes the essential human element from the race of Adam, but this human element is free from sin due to her immaculate conception. She was enabled by a singular grace of God, "by reason of the merits of her Son" (CCC 491), to overcome her human limitations and give birth to Christ, the New Adam. "Mary is thus enabled to do what, outside of this grace, no human creature ever could, Mother into being the very person of the Incarnate Son."[102]

---

[102]   "Mary's Role in the Incarnation," *Communio*, 30 (Spring 2003), 5–25.

St. Thomas Aquinas conveys something of the wonder of Mary's role in the incarnation of the Son of God in human flesh: "The soul of the holy Virgin was so filled with grace that from her soul grace poured into her flesh from which was conceived the Son of God. Hugh of St. Victor says of this: 'Because the love of the Holy Spirit so inflamed her soul, He worked a wonder in her flesh, in that from it was born God made Man.' 'And therefore also the Holy which shall be born of you shall be called the Son of God' (Lk 1:3)."[103]

We must never forget that it is from the Blessed Virgin Mary that Christ takes his sacred humanity. And it is through his sacred humanity that we are able to participate in Christ's mysteries and receive their graces. Blessed Columba Marmion explains the importance of Mary: "No piety would be truly Christian if it did not include in its object the Mother of the Incarnate Word. Devotion towards the Virgin Mary is not only important, but necessary, if we wish to draw abundantly at the source of life. To separate Christ from His Mother in our piety, is to divide Christ; it is to lose sight of the essential mission of His Sacred Humanity in the distribution of Divine grace. Where the Mother is left out, the Son is no longer understood."[104]

The Blessed Virgin Mary continues to have a unique role in our supernatural life of grace by virtue of being the mother of the Redeemer and Co-Redemptrix. Pope Leo XIII

---

[103]   Thomas Aquinas, *The Angelic Salutation*, https://isidore.co/aquinas/english/AveMaria.htm.
[104]   Dom Columba Marmion, *Christ the Life of the Soul* (London: Sands & C0, 1925), 340.

taught in his encyclical *Octobri Mense* on the Rosary of the grace which is given to us through Mary, such being the Divine Will: "Thus through her are granted all the graces men need, in their different conditions and stages of life. It has been so for twenty centuries: it will remain so till the end of time. Mary obtains for us all we need for our journey towards eternity."[105]

A number of saints have used maternal imagery to describe the intimate role of Mary in bestowing on them the graces necessary for Christ to be "born" in their hearts: Blessed Columba Marmion writes, "She will hear our prayer; we shall have the immense joy of seeing Christ born anew within our hearts by the communication of a more abundant grace."[106] St. Teresa Benedicta of the Cross (Edith Stein), the Carmelite martyr of Auschwitz, wrote a poem addressed to Our Lord, December 24, 1936:

> My heart has become Your manger,
> Awaiting You,
> But not for long!
> Maria, Your mother and also mine
> Has given me her name.
> At midnight she will place her newborn child
> Into my heart.[107]

---

[105]   Reginald Garrigou-Lagrange, *The Mother of the Saviour* (Charlotte: TAN Books, 1993), 207–8.

[106]   Dom Columba Marmion, *Christ in His Mysteries* (London: Sands & Co, 1939), 113.

[107]   *Edith Stein: Selected Writings. With Comments, Reminiscences and Translations of her Prayers and Poems by her niece Susanne M. Batzdorff* (Springfield: Templegate Publishers, 1990), 61.

Blessed Titus Brandsma, the Carmelite martyr of Dachau, exhorts us to "unite ourselves to Mary, so that God should be conceived in us also, and brought forth by us. It is our task to bear God as she bore Him."[108]

Asking for the intercession of St. Teresa Benedicta of the Cross, Blessed Titus Brandsma, and Blessed Columba Marmion, we must pray that Mary, our Mother, bestows on us the grace to imitate her Son, the New Adam, in order to transform our grief in the light of heaven.

Living Our Grief From the Perspective of Heaven

Though we cannot assume that our loved ones have gone to heaven—this would be to presume on the mercy of God—we can see their deaths from the perspective of heaven. St. Faustina gives us grounds for hope about the final destiny of our loved ones, even those who in life seemingly rejected the Faith. This entry in her diary explains what happens at the moment of death:

> I often attend upon the dying and through entreaties obtain for them trust in God's mercy, and I implore God for an abundance of divine grace, which is always victorious. God's mercy sometimes touches the sinner at the last moment in a wondrous and mysterious way. Outwardly, it seems as if everything were lost, but it is not so. The soul, illumined by a ray of God's powerful final grace, turns to God in the last moment with such a power of love that, in an instant, it receives

---

[108] Rev. Nick Donnelly, *Our Journey to Christmas* (London: Catholic Truth Society, 2016) 60.

from God forgiveness of sin and punishment, while outwardly it shows no sign either of repentance or of contrition, because souls [at that stage] no longer react to external things. Oh, how beyond comprehension is God's mercy! But—horror!—there are also souls who voluntarily and consciously reject and scorn this grace! Although a person is at the point of death, the merciful God gives the soul that interior vivid moment, so that if the soul is willing, it has the possibility of returning to God. (Diary 1698)

St. Faustina also shows that those who live, from the perspective of heaven, know the true value of the traditional devotion of indulgences, which has been so sadly neglected in recent years. There was once a universal understanding among the faithful about how we can help the souls of our loved ones, and others, through indulgences. Our Lord told St. Faustina of the importance of indulgences to help the souls suffering the purifying fires of purgatory:

Today bring to Me the souls who are in the prison of Purgatory and immerse them in the abyss of My mercy. Let the torrents of My Blood cool down their scorching flames. All these souls are greatly loved by Me. They are making retribution to My justice. It is in your power to bring them relief. Draw all the indulgences from the treasury of My Church and offer them on their behalf. Oh, if you only knew the torments they suffer, you would continually offer for them the alms of the spirit and pay off their debt to My justice. (Diary 1226)

The *Baltimore Catechism* explains why indulgences were such a popular devotion for the faithful who wanted to continue to show loving solicitude for their loved ones after death: "The word indulgence means a favor or concession. An indulgence obtains by a very slight penance the remission of penalties that would otherwise be severe" (840). Indulgences can be gained for oneself or for souls in purgatory by intentionally offering up a Mass, prayer, or even personal suffering. Cecily Hallack, the English Catholic author, gave a beautiful explanation of indulgences in her children's book *Adventure of The Amethyst:*

> And if I was so pleased at your helping each other, how much more must God be pleased when we help each other! Now about vicarious suffering. We can do things and ask God to count them as done by someone who hasn't much to give Him — someone who may appear before Him as an untrustworthy servant. But of course there is the chance that people who have not trusted and obeyed God, but have given in to the devil and done harm and made trouble, may be in such a bad temper that they won't accept our offering. . . . But there is one kind of souls whom we are quite sure won't say that, and those are the dead whom we call the Holy Souls. Those who did try to trust and obey God, but who didn't leave their own will *completely* and who don't want to enter heaven with that stain of selfishness on them. They can only serve God after death by waiting until they have made up in sorrow and patience and suffering what they left undone or

have not made enough amends for sin. It is so awful to see the harm that selfishness does in the world — how it spoils God's plan, and makes Him sad, and other people suffer, and stains the beauty of the soul, that they suffer a fire of suffering. But that fire of suffering burns up the stain, just as a fire in the garden burns up rubbish. Well, of course, they won't refuse our offerings to them! And God loves few things better than for us to share our good deeds with them, and especially to pray for them. It is an old Breton custom to put flowers on graves on All Souls' Day, because on that day we make them such a great feast of offerings and prayers that many of them are able to go to heaven, because our offerings have made up what they didn't do."[109]

Part of the pain of grief is the sense of powerlessness that we feel, assuming that we are unable to help our loved ones once they have died. Practicing the devotion of indulgences for their souls, and the souls of others, is a great solace and channels all our suffering and struggle to a positive purpose. (An appendix to this book explains the conditions required for different types of indulgences).

The Imitation of Christ

Nowadays it's necessary to explain the meaning of "imitation" as a devotional practice because modern usage of the word can mean an intentional fraud or counterfeit meant to

---

[109]   Cecily Hallack, *Adventure of The Amethyst* (London: Macmillan & Co. Ltd, 1945), 234–35.

deceive. In Christian discipleship, *Imitatio Christi*—the Imitation of Christ—means the working of grace conforming us to be like Christ in our personalities, thinking, and way of living.

St. Paul understands the Christian life to be the working out of God's providence in our lives conforming us to become an image of Christ, "For those whom he foreknew he also predestined to be conformed to the image of his Son, in order that he might be the firstborn within a large family" (Rom 8:29). He described himself as an imitator of Christ: "Be imitators of me, as I am of Christ" (1 Cor 11:1). St. Paul therefore saw the imitation of God as summing up the way of Christian discipleship: "Therefore be imitators of God, as beloved children, and live in love, as Christ loved us and gave himself up for us, a fragrant offering and sacrifice to God"(Eph 5:1).

Likewise, St. Augustine sees the imitation of Christ as the essence of Christian discipleship, as the primary means to overcome man's primal sin of self-sufficient pride: "Why are you proud, O man? God, for you, became low. You would perhaps be ashamed to imitate a lowly man; at any rate, imitate the lowly God. The Son of God came in the character of a man and was made low."[110]

Augustine also recommends the imitation of Christ as the means for us to stop shaping ourselves by the standards of this world, helping us tame the "wild beasts" of the living soul.[111]

---

[110]   St. Augustine, "Tractates on the Gospel of John," 25, https://www. newadvent.org/fathers/1701025.htm.

[111]   *The Works of Saint Augustine: A Translation for the 21st Century. The*

Thomas à Kempis, in his devotional work *The Imitation of Christ*, presents the *imitatio Christi* as the means of escaping the evils of this world:

> "He who follows Me, walks not in darkness," says the Lord. John 8:12. By these words of Christ we are advised to imitate His life and habits, if we wish to be truly enlightened and free from all blindness of heart. Let our chief effort, therefore, be to study the life of Jesus Christ. The teaching of Christ is more excellent than all the advice of the saints, and he who has His spirit will find in it a hidden manna. Now, there are many who hear the Gospel often but care little for it because they have not the spirit of Christ. Yet whoever wishes to understand fully the words of Christ must try to pattern his whole life on that of Christ.[112]

The imitation of Christ—making Christ the pattern of our whole life—will help us find the hidden manna in the desert of our grief.

Salvific Suffering and the Theology of the Imitation of Christ

Recovering from the protracted injuries inflicted on him as a consequence of the assassination attempt against his life in 1981, Pope St. John Paul II composed a theology of the imitation of the suffering Christ. It helps us see how sharing

---

Confessions (New York: New City Press, 1997), 364.

[112]   Thomas à Kempis, *The Imitation of Christ*, Book 1, chap. 1, http://www.documentacatholicaomnia.eu/03d/1380-1471,_Kempis._Thomas,_The_Imitation_Of_Christ,_EN.pdf.

Christ's paschal mystery transforms and gives eternal value to our own suffering.

Pope St. John Paul II's starting point is the mystery par excellence of the mysteries of Christ—the redemption of mankind by the paschal mystery of Christ. Christ the Redeemer suffered for every person; therefore, every person is united to the suffering of Christ. Due to this inextricable union between Christ in his suffering and each one of us in our suffering, "one can say that with the Passion of Christ all human suffering has found itself in a new situation."[113]

The Son of God allows a mysterious exchange between his suffering on the cross and each one of us in our sufferings: "The Redeemer suffered in place of man and for man. Every man has his own share in the Redemption. Each one is also called to share in that suffering through which the Redemption was accomplished. He is called to share in that suffering through which all human suffering has also been redeemed. In bringing about the Redemption through suffering, Christ has also raised human suffering to the level of the Redemption. Thus each man, in his suffering, can also become a sharer in the redemptive suffering of Christ."[114]

This supernatural exchange is possible only because "Christ has opened his suffering to man" due to his redemptive suffering making him "a sharer in all human sufferings."

Christ's suffering on the cross presents us with a model to understand and persevere through the trials of our own

---

[113]   Pope St. John Paul II, *Salvifici Doloris*, 19, http://www.vatican.va/content/john-paul-ii/en/apost_letters/1984/documents/hf_jp-ii_apl_11021984_salvifici-doloris.html.

[114]   Ibid.

suffering, expressed as the interrelated paradoxes of the cross and the Resurrection, weakness and strength, degradation and glorification, sinking down and rising up: "Those who share in Christ's sufferings have before their eyes the Paschal Mystery of the Cross and Resurrection, in which Christ descends, in a first phase, to the ultimate limits of human weakness and impotence: indeed, he dies nailed to the Cross. But if at the same time in this weakness there is accomplished his lifting up, confirmed by the power of the Resurrection, then this means that the weaknesses of all human sufferings are capable of being infused with the same power of God manifested in Christ's Cross."[115]

Through his incarnation, and especially through his paschal mystery, Christ created a new type of suffering—salvific suffering—which he invites us to share with him for the redemption of mankind. This means embracing as his divine will for our lives, our experiences of weakness and emptiness, the epitome of which is grief: "To suffer means to become particularly susceptible, particularly open to the working of the salvific powers of God, offered to humanity in Christ. In him God has confirmed his desire to act especially through suffering, which is man's weakness and emptying of self, and he wishes to make his power known precisely in this weakness and emptying of self. This also explains the exhortation in the First Letter of Peter: 'Yet if one suffers as a Christian, let him not be ashamed, but under that name let him glorify God.'"[116]

---

[115]   Ibid., 23.
[116]   Ibid.

As Christians, we are called to become sharers in the sufferings of Christ, which means that through faith and the sacraments, we discover the redemptive sufferings of Christ, and through the mysterious exchange on the cross, we discover our own sufferings are, through faith, "enriched with a new content and new meaning"[117]—our suffering, united with Christ's suffering, becomes a creative force for good in the world: "The sufferings of Christ created the good of the world's redemption. This good in itself is inexhaustible and infinite. No man can add anything to it. But at the same time, in the mystery of the Church as his Body, Christ has in a sense opened his own redemptive suffering to all human suffering. In so far as man becomes a sharer in Christ's sufferings—in any part of the world and at any time in history—to that extent he in his own way completes the suffering through which Christ accomplished the Redemption of the world."[118]

Our union with the salvific sufferings of Christ not only benefit the world, they benefit us profoundly on the way of Christian perfection, enabling us to attain spiritual maturity in two ways: salvific suffering enables us to "manifest the moral greatness of man," as we see the countless martyrs down the ages, and it leads to the "spiritual tempering of man":

> Suffering as it were contains a special call to the virtue which man must exercise on his own part. And this is the virtue of perseverance in bearing whatever

---

[117]   Ibid., 20.
[118]   Ibid., 24.

disturbs and causes harm. In doing this, the individual unleashes hope, which maintains in him the conviction that suffering will not get the better of him, that it will not deprive him of his dignity as a human being, a dignity linked to awareness of the meaning of life. And indeed this meaning makes itself known together with the working of God's love, which is the supreme gift of the Holy Spirit. The more he shares in this love, man rediscovers himself more and more fully in suffering: he rediscovers the "soul" which he thought he had "lost" because of suffering.[119]

Devotions that Help the Imitation of Christ During Times of Emergency

Thomas à Kempis

Thomas à Kempis, in Christianity's greatest work on the imitation of Christ, advocates to those who seek to imitate Christ that we foster an ardent devotion to the Blessed Sacrament. Through adoration of the Blessed Sacrament, we "enact the work of redemption and become a sharer in all the merits of Christ." If you are not able to physically come before the Blessed Sacrament, close your eyes and call to mind the monstrance containing Christ's most precious Body and make Thomas à Kempis's prayer and thought on Eucharistic adoration your own:

> You, the Lord of the universe, Who have need of nothing, have willed to dwell in us by means of Your

---

[119]   Ibid., 23.

Sacrament. Keep my heart and body clean, so that with a joyous and spotless conscience I may be able often to celebrate Your Mysteries and to receive for my eternal salvation what You have ordained and instituted for Your special honor and as an everlasting memorial.

Rejoice, my soul, and give thanks to God for having left you so noble a gift and so special a consolation in this valley of tears. As often as you renew this Mystery and receive the Body of Christ, so often do you enact the work of redemption and become a sharer in all the merits of Christ, for the love of Christ never grows less and the wealth of His mercy is never exhausted.

Therefore, you should prepare yourself for it by constantly renewing your heart and pondering deeply the great mystery of salvation. As often as you celebrate or hear Mass, it should seem as great, as new, as sweet to you as if on that very day Christ became man in the womb of the Virgin, or, hanging on the Cross, suffered and died for the salvation of man.[120]

St. John Henry Newman

Cardinal Newman spent time every day in adoration of Our Lord in the Blessed Sacrament, profoundly aware of Our Lord's living presence, "He is not past, He is present now. And though He is not seen, He is here. The same God who walked the water, who did miracles, etc., is in the Tabernacle. We come before Him, we speak to Him just as He was spoken to 1800 years ago, etc."[121] Cardinal Newman

---

[120] Thomas à Kempis, *The Imitation of Christ*, Book Four, chap. 2.

[121] Blessed John Henry Newman, *Sermon Notes* (London: Longmans,

composed this Eucharistic meditation, using the "O" antiphons of Advent to meditate on a different mystery of Jesus each day:

A Short Visit to the Blessed Sacrament
Before Meditation[122]

During an emergency, you may be unable to be physically present before the tabernacle or monstrance, but you can still pay a short visit to the Blessed Sacrament spiritually, directing your prayers to the nearest Catholic tabernacle:

In the Name of the Father, and of the Son, and of the Holy Spirit. Amen.

I place myself in the presence of Him, in whose Incarnate Presence I am before I place myself there.

I adore Thee, O my Savior, present here as God and man, in soul and body, in true flesh and blood.

I acknowledge and confess that I kneel before that Sacred Humanity, which was conceived in Mary's womb, and lay in Mary's bosom; which grew up to man's estate, and by the Sea of Galilee called the Twelve, wrought miracles, and spoke words of wisdom and peace; which in due season hung on the cross, lay in the tomb, rose from the dead, and now reigns in heaven.

Greens & Co, 1913), 90.

[122] "A Short Visit to the Blessed Sacrament before Meditation," http://www.newmanreader.org/works/meditations/meditations9. html#top.

I praise, and bless, and give myself wholly to Him, who is the true Bread of my soul, and my everlasting joy.

Sunday

O Wisdom, You come out of the mouth of the Most High, reaching from end to end, with might and gentleness ordering all things. O come and teach us the way of prudence.

Monday

O Adonai, and leader of the house of Israel, You appeared to Moses in the fire of the burning bush, and You gave him the Law on Sinai. O come and redeem us with arm outstretched.

Tuesday

O root of Jesse, You are an ensign of the peoples, at whom the kings shall shut their mouths, whom all the people shall beseech. O come to deliver us, and do not delay.

Wednesday

O key of David, and scepter of the house of Israel, what You open, no man can shut; what You shut, no man can open. O come and lead forth the prisoner from the prison-house, and him that sit in darkness, and in the shadow of death.

Thursday

O Dayspring, You are the splendor of the light eternal and the sun of justice. O come and enlighten them that sit in darkness and the shadow of death.

Friday

O King and desire of all peoples, You are the cornerstone that makes those who are divided into one. O come to save man, whom You made from the mud of the earth.

Saturday

O Emmanuel, our King and Lawgiver, the One whom the people long for, and their Savior. O come and save us, Lord our God.

The Imitation of Mary

There is a long and ancient tradition going back to the Fathers of the Church of encouraging the imitation of Mary, as the preeminent exemplar among the saints of the graces and virtues essential for Christian perfection. Bishop Alexander of Alexandria writes, "You have the conduct of Mary, who is the type and image of the life that is proper to heaven."[123] St. Ambrose taught that Mary's life is a rule of life for all: "From this you may take your pattern of life, showing, as an example, the clear rules of virtue: what you have to correct, to effect, and to hold fast."[124] Pope Leo XIII points to the human nature that we share in common as creatures

---

[123]   Michael O'Carroll, *Theotokos: A Theological Encyclopedia of the Blessed Virgin Mary* (Collegeville: A Michael Glazier Book, 1982), 178.

[124]   Philip Schaff, "Ambrose: Selected Works and Letters," Book 2, chap. 2, http://www.documentacatholicaomnia.eu/03d/0339-0397,_Ambrosius,_De_Virginibus_Ad_Marcellinam_Sororem_Sua_Libri_Tres_[Schaff],_EN.pdf.

with Mary as the source of her attractiveness as an exemplar to imitate:

> In Mary we see how a truly good and provident God has established for us a most suitable example of every virtue. As we look upon her and think about her we are not cast down as though stricken by the overpowering splendor of God's power; but, on the contrary, attracted by the closeness of the common nature we share with her, we strive with greater confidence to imitate her. If we, with her powerful help, should dedicate ourselves wholly and entirely to this undertaking, we can portray at least an outline of such great virtue and sanctity, and reproducing that perfect conformity of our lives to all God's designs which she possessed in so marvelous a degree, we shall follow her into heaven.[125]

Pope Leo XIII highlights an essential feature of Mary's role as the preeminent exemplar among the saints, not only has she been established by God for our imitation, but she dispenses "powerful help" to assist us in imitating her great virtue and sanctity.

These powerful graces dispensed by Our Lady are the reason why she is venerated as the Mother of Christians and tradition honors her spiritual maternity of souls in heaven. The source of her spiritual maternity can be traced back to Our Lord's words from the cross addressed to his mother

---

[125] Pope Leo XIII, *Magnae Dei Matris*, 26, http://www.vatican.va/content/leo-xiii/en/encyclicals/documents/hf_l-xiii_enc_08091892_magnae-dei-matris.html.

and St. John, "Woman, here is your son." Then he said to the disciple, "Here is your mother" (Jn 19:26–27). Father Reginald Garrigou-Lagrange, OP, explains the traditional understanding of Jesus's words: they "do not refer to a grace peculiar to St. John alone, but go beyond him to all who are to be regenerated by the Cross." And regarding Mary, "the words of the dying Savior, like sacramental words, produce what they signify: in Mary's soul they produced a great increase of charity and of maternal love for us. . . . Mary continues to exercise her motherly functions in our regard by watching over us so that we grow in charity and persevere in it, by interceding for us and by distributing to us all the graces we receive."[126]

Out of her maternal love for us, Mary shows special care during the times we suffer, especially during times of grief, because she is particularly acquainted with the sorrow of grief due to her witness of her Son's passion and death on the cross.

The Theology of Our Lady's Compassion

The theology of Our Lady's compassion begins with Simeon's prophecy about her at Jesus's presentation in the Temple: "and a sword will pierce your own soul too" (Lk 2:35). By these words God decrees that Mary would intimately cooperate in the redemptive suffering and death of her Son. St. Alphonsus Liguori summarizes the understanding of the Church Fathers and saints of this piercing of Our Lady's

---

[126]   Reginald Garrigou-Lagrange, *The Mother of the Saviour* (Charlotte: TAN Books, 1993), 155–56.

soul, which they identified as occurring at the same time as
Our Lord's heart was pierced by the spear:

> The Holy Fathers explain this to be the very sword
> predicted to the Virgin by St. Simeon; a sword, not of
> iron, but of grief, which pierced through her blessed
> soul in the heart of Jesus, where it always dwelt. Thus,
> among others, St. Bernard says: "The spear which
> opened his side passed through the soul of the Virgin,
> which could not be torn from the heart of Jesus." And
> the divine mother herself revealed the same to St. Brid-
> get, saying: "When the spear was drawn out, the point
> appeared red with blood; then I felt as if my heart were
> pierced when I saw the heart of my most dear Son
> pierced." The angel told St. Bridget, that such were
> the sufferings of Mary, that she was saved from death
> only by the miraculous power of God. In her other
> dolors she at least had her Son to compassionate her;
> and now she had not even him to take pity on her.[127]

God willed that Mary intimately share in her spirit the
redemptive sufferings her Son endured—body, soul, and
spirit—on the cross. In this way, Mary uniquely cooper-
ated with the Son of God's redemption of mankind, and
as such, her compassion at the foot of the cross has an eternal redemptive merit and significance. Cardinal Newman
describes the different ways Jesus and Mary shared in his
passion: "But He, Who bore the sinner's shame for sinners,
spared His Mother, who was sinless, this supreme indignity.

---

[127]   St. Alphonsus Liguori, *The Glories of Mary* (Liguori: Liguori Pub-
lications, 2000), 320.

Not in the body, but in the soul, she suffered a fellow-passion; she was crucified with Him; the spear that pierced His breast pierced through her soul."[128]

Cardinal Newman describes Mary's spiritual suffering as sharing in the "acutest part" of Jesus's suffering, which was on the level of intellect, the spiritual faculty of man that is made in the image and likeness of God: "He was to save us by that Body and Blood which she furnished; not she. He was to be made a sacrament for us as well as a sacrifice. Yet she was privileged to share the *acutest* part of His sufferings, the mental, once she came into the midst, at His Crucifixion. Mental pain all in a moment, like a spear; despondency; sinking of nerves; no support. Yet she stood."[129]

The little detail in the Gospel that Mary stood at the foot of the cross (Jn 19:25) has eternal significance according to Cardinal Newman, showing her willing and active cooperation in the redemptive sacrifice of her Son: "It is expressly noted of her that she stood by the Cross. She did not grovel in the dust, but stood upright to receive the blows, the stabs, which the long Passion of her Son inflicted upon her every moment. In this magnanimity and generosity in suffering she is, as compares with the Apostles, fitly imaged as a Tower."[130]

---

[128]   Nicholas L. Gregoris, *The Daughter of Eve Unfallen: Mary in the Theology and Spirituality of John Henry Newman* (Mount Pocono: Newman House Press, 2003), 338.

[129]   Blessed John Henry Newman, *Sermon Notes* (London: Longmans, Greens & Co, 1913), 63.

[130]   John Henry Newman, *Meditations and Devotions: Meditations on the Litany of Loreto, for the Month of May,* http://www.newman-reader.org/works/meditations/meditations2.html#may21.

Cardinal Newman calls us to greatly esteem and value the courage and strength of Our Lady standing at the foot of the cross, enduring her hidden, silent, spiritual "fellow-passion" alongside her Son: "Yet here were no visible signs of this intimate martyrdom; she stood up, still, collected, motionless, solitary, under the Cross of her Son, surrounded by Angels, and shrouded in her virginal sanctity from the notice of all who were taking part in His Crucifixion."[131]

For all these reasons, Mary can help us by her example and graces to transform our grief over the death of loved ones into a "fellow passion" with her Son, cooperating in the redemption of mankind. And as our spiritual Mother, Mary will also console us in our grief. St. John Henry Newman explains the rightness of Our Lady having the title *Consolatrix Afflictorum*, "Consoler of the Afflicted," as originating in her suffering at the foot of the cross, "This is the secret of true consolation: those are able to comfort others who, in their own case, have been much tried, and have felt the need of consolation, and have received it."[132]

Mary Invites Us to Share Her Compassion for Sinners

An expression of Mary's continuing cooperation in the redemptive sufferings of her Son on the cross is her maternal concern for sinners, expressed time and again during her apparitions. She invites us to share her compassion for sinners by making acts of reparation for their sins and our own sins. She helps us gain an awareness of the deep offence and anger God has towards sin.

---

[131]   Ibid.
[132]   Ibid.

Heaven's command that we make reparations for sin was the major message of the apparitions of Fatima. The angel of Portugal's apparition to the children prepared them to receive Our Lady's message about reparation. The angel instructed the children to pray the following, telling them,

> Pray thus. The Hearts of Jesus and Mary are attentive to the voices of your supplications. . . .

> My God, I believe, I adore, I hope and I love You! I ask pardon of You for those who do not believe, do not adore, do not hope and do not love You.[133]

In preparation for the apparitions of Our Lady, the angel also instructed them to make a further act of reparation before the Blessed Sacrament, which was made supernaturally present to the kneeling children:

> Most Holy Trinity, Father, Son and Holy Spirit, I adore You profoundly, and I offer You the most precious Body, Blood, Soul and Divinity of Jesus Christ, present in all the tabernacles of the world, in reparation for the outrages, sacrileges and indifference with which He Himself is offended. And, through the infinite merits of His most Sacred Heart, and the Immaculate Heart of Mary, I beg You the conversion of poor sinners.[134]

The children took to heart the angel's message of reparation, accepting any sufferings that came their way with a prayer

---

133   Lucia Santos, *Fatima in Lucia's Own Words: Sister Lucia's Memoirs* (Fatima: Secretariado Dos Pastorinhos, 2007), 78.

134   Ibid., 79.

that they composed themselves, "My God, it is as an act of reparation, and for the conversion of sinners, that we offer You all these sufferings and sacrifices."[135]

During her apparitions, Our Lady taught the children the importance and necessity of reparation for sin by showing them a vision of hell. She told them: "Sacrifice yourselves for sinners, and say many times, especially whenever you make some sacrifice: O Jesus, it is for love of You, for the conversion of sinners, and in reparation for the sins committed against the Immaculate Heart of Mary. . . . You have seen hell where the souls of poor sinners go. To save them, God wishes to establish in the world devotion to my Immaculate Heart. If what I say to you is done, many souls will be saved and there will be peace."[136]

To this end, Our Lady gave two more appeals to acts of reparation to the children, and ourselves, requesting that we make Communions of Reparation on five consecutive first Saturdays and that we add this prayer after each Mystery of the Most Holy Rosary:

> "O my Jesus, forgive us, save us from the fire of hell.
> Lead all souls to Heaven, especially those who are
> most in need."[137]

Sometime after the original apparitions, Our Lady, appeared with the child Jesus to Sister Lucia again emphasizing that making reparations for sin was a special way of showing love for her. In the apparition, the child Jesus said, "Have

---

135   Ibid., 81.
136   Ibid., 178.
137   Ibid., 179.

pity on the Heart of your Most Holy Mother. It is covered with thorns with which ungrateful men pierce it at every moment, and there is no one to make an act of reparation to remove them."[138]

Grief over the death of loved ones, particularly if they died during an emergency, can be the greatest suffering of our lives. Our Lady invites us, when we are ready, to make such grief into an act of reparation for the sake of sinners, and for our own sin. In this way, grace can transform our grief into redemptive suffering united to the suffering of Christ and his mother.

Reparations for the Sins of the Dead

The Church also teaches that we can make reparations as indulgences for the sins of our loved ones who have died:

> This teaching is also based on the practice of prayer for the dead, already mentioned in Sacred Scripture: "Therefore [Judas Maccabeus] made atonement for the dead, that they might be delivered from their sin." From the beginning the Church has honored the memory of the dead and offered prayers in suffrage for them, above all the Eucharistic sacrifice, so that, thus purified, they may attain the beatific vision of God. The Church also commends almsgiving, indulgences, and works of penance undertaken on behalf of the dead: "Let us help and commemorate them. If Job's sons were purified by their father's sacrifice, why

---

138   "Fatima and the Five First Saturday's devotion," https://www. olqp.net/world-apostolate-of-fatima-in-england-and-wales.

would we doubt that our offerings for the dead bring them some consolation? Let us not hesitate to help those who have died and to offer our prayers for them" (St. John Chrysostom). (CCC 1032)

It is a great solace to know that the intense suffering of our grief can be put to use as a sacrifice of reparation that will help our loved ones attain the beatific vision if they are in purgatory.

Devotions that Help the Imitation of Mary During Times of Emergency

The Memorare

This is the preeminent traditional prayer that expresses our filial trust that Mary will help us during an emergency with a mother's concern and urgency, our heavenly mother given us by Our Lord Jesus Christ:

> Remember, O most loving Virgin Mary, that it is a thing unheard of, that anyone ever had recourse to your protection, implored your help, or sought your intercession, and was left forsaken. Filled therefore with confidence in your goodness I fly to you, O Mother, Virgin of virgins. To you I come, before you I stand, a sorrowful sinner. Despise not my poor words, O Mother of the Word of God, but graciously hear and grant my prayer. Amen.

Devotions to Our Lady of Sorrows

Devotions to the *Mater Dolorosa* (Mother of Sorrows), also known as Our Lady of Sorrows, are traditional ways the faithful express their imitation of Mary, seeking to join our sufferings with hers, and asking for the grace of her consolation. Professor Eamon Duffy explains the origins of these devotions in the Middle Ages:

> As it developed in the later Middle Ages the cult of the Sorrows of the Virgin, or the Mater Dolorosa, had a variety of functions, high among them that of serving as an objective correlative for the discharge of grief and suffering in the face of successive waves of plague sweeping through Christendom. . . . The essence of the devotion was that evident in what is arguably its noblest expression, the "Stabat Mater". Here the Virgin's grief is presented, not as an end in itself, but as a means of arousing and focusing sympathetic suffering in the heart of the onlooker. In this literal compassion, this identification with the sufferings of Christ by sharing the grief of his Mother, lay salvation.[139]

The Rosary of the Seven Sorrows

The Rosary of the Seven Sorrows, otherwise known as the Chaplet of Seven Sorrows or the Servite Rosary, has been a popular means of meditating on the sorrows that pierced the heart of the Blessed Virgin Mary. The seven sorrows of Our Lady are the prophecy of Simeon, the flight into Egypt,

---

[139] Eamon Duffy, *The Stripping of the Altars* (New Haven: Yale University Press, 1992), 259.

losing the Holy Child at Jerusalem, meeting her Son on his way to Calvary, standing at the foot of the cross, her Son placed in her arms after being taken from the cross, and the burial of Christ.

How to pray the Rosary of the Seven Sorrows

1. Sign of the Cross and an act of contrition.
2. Announce one of the Seven Sorrows, then pray the Our Father.
3. Pray seven Hail Mary's while meditating on the Sorrow.
4. At the conclusion of each sorrow, pray: Holy Mother hear my prayers, and renew in my heart each wound of Jesus my Savior.
5. Repeat all Seven Sorrows.
6. Pray three Hail Mary's in honor of the sacred tears of Our Sorrowful Mother.
7. Concluding prayers: V. Pray for us, O most sorrowful Virgin. R. That we may be made worthy of the promises of Christ.

O Mary, you truly became the Queen of all martyrs as these seven bitter swords of sorrow pierced your immaculate heart! By the merit of your tearful distress obtain for us and for all sinners the grace of perfect contrition and conversion. Help us always, dear Mother, to imitate you by taking up our crosses and following Jesus with limitless love and generosity. Amen.

It was revealed to St. Bridget of Sweden that devotion to the Blessed Virgin Mary's Seven Sorrows will bring great graces.

St. Bonaventure's Prayer to Our Lady of Sorrows

O most Holy Virgin, Mother of our Lord Jesus Christ: by the overwhelming grief you experienced when you witnessed the martyrdom, the crucifixion, and the death of your divine Son, look upon me with eyes of compassion and awaken in my heart a tender commiseration for those sufferings, as well as a sincere detestation of my sins, in order that, being disengaged from all undue affections for the passing joys of this earth, I may long for the eternal Jerusalem, and that henceforth all my thoughts and all my actions may be directed toward this one most desirable object. Honor, glory, and love to our divine Lord Jesus, and to the holy and immaculate mother of God. Amen.

The Fatima Chaplet of Adoration and Reparation

This chaplet is based on the prayers of reparation given to the children at Fatima by the angel of Portugal. Pray this chaplet in reparation for the sins committed by your loved ones to help them in purgatory, for other souls in purgatory, and for your own sins.

Begin your Rosary as usual—Apostles Creed, one Our Father, three Hail Mary's for faith, hope, and charity, the Act of Contrition.

On the large beads:

> Most Holy Trinity, Father, Son, and Holy Spirit,
> I adore you profoundly, and I
> offer You the Most Precious Body, Blood,
> Soul and Divinity of Jesus Christ,

present in all the tabernacles of the
world, in reparation for the outrages,
sacrileges, and indifference by which
He is offended, and by the infinite
merits of His Most Sacred Heart and
through the Immaculate Heart of Mary,
I beg the conversion of poor sinners. Amen.

On the small beads:

My God, I believe, I adore, I hope and I love You!
I ask pardon for those who do not believe,
do not adore, do not hope and do not love You.
   Amen.

Finish each decade with one Glory Be (and)

O Most Holy Trinity, I adore You!
My God, My God, I love You in the most
Blessed Sacrament. Amen.

It's common nowadays in any treatment or mention of grief
for people to talk about "seeking closure." Attaining such a
state of closure is presented as the positive end goal of grief.
But closure is not what Catholics seek through our prayers,
devotions, and indulgences for Holy souls, because our relationship with the dead doesn't come to an end. Instead of
closure, we seek consummation—the consummation of
our loved ones' eternal destiny, and our own eventual consummation after death. And what is this consummation?
It is the consummation of our faith, hope, and love in the
beatific vision, the ultimate experience of *imitatio Dei*, the

"imitation of God." "Beloved, we are God's children now; what we will be has not yet been revealed. What we do know is this: when he is revealed, we will be like him, for we will see him as he is" (1 Jn 3:2).

More Devotions that Help the Imitation of Jesus and the Imitation of Mary

Litany of the Holy Name of Jesus

Lord, have mercy on us.

Christ, have mercy on us.

Lord, have mercy on us. Jesus, hear us.

Jesus, graciously hear us.

God the Father of Heaven

Have mercy on us.

God the Son, Redeemer of the world,

Have mercy on us.

God the Holy Spirit,

Have mercy on us.

Holy Trinity, one God,

Have mercy on us.

Jesus, Son of the living God, R. Have mercy on us.

Jesus, splendor of the Father, [etc.]

Jesus, brightness of eternal light.

Jesus, King of glory.

Jesus, sun of justice.

Jesus, Son of the Virgin Mary.

Jesus, most amiable.

Jesus, most admirable.

Jesus, the mighty God.

Jesus, Father of the world to come.

Jesus, angel of great counsel.

Jesus, most powerful.

Jesus, most patient.

Jesus, most obedient.

Jesus, meek and humble of heart.

Jesus, lover of chastity.

Jesus, lover of us.

Jesus, God of peace.

Jesus, author of life.

Jesus, example of virtues.

Jesus, zealous lover of souls.

Jesus, our God.

Jesus, our refuge.

Jesus, father of the poor.

Jesus, treasure of the faithful.

Jesus, good Shepherd.

Jesus, true light.

Jesus, eternal wisdom.

Jesus, infinite goodness.

Jesus, our way and our life.

Jesus, joy of Angels.

Jesus, King of the Patriarchs.

Jesus, Master of the Apostles.

Jesus, teacher of the Evangelists.

Jesus, strength of Martyrs.

Jesus, light of Confessors.

Jesus, purity of Virgins.

Jesus, crown of Saints.

Be merciful, spare us, O Jesus.
Be merciful, graciously hear us, O Jesus.

From all evil, deliver us, O Jesus.
From all sin, deliver us, O Jesus.
From Your wrath, [etc.]
From the snares of the devil.
From the spirit of fornication.
From everlasting death.
From the neglect of Your inspirations.
By the mystery of Your holy Incarnation.
By Your Nativity.
By Your Infancy.
By Your most divine Life.
By Your labors.
By Your agony and passion.
By Your cross and dereliction.
By Your sufferings.
By Your death and burial.
By Your Resurrection.
By Your Ascension.
By Your institution of the most Holy Eucharist.
By Your joys.
By Your glory.

Lamb of God, who takes away the sins of the world,
spare us, O Jesus.
Lamb of God, who takes away the sins of the world,
graciously hear us, O Jesus.
Lamb of God, who takes away the sins of the world,
have mercy on us, O Jesus.

Jesus, hear us.

Jesus, graciously hear us.

Let us pray.

O Lord Jesus Christ, You have said, "Ask and you shall receive, seek, and you shall find, knock, and it shall be opened to you." Grant, we beg of You, to us who ask it, the gift of Your most divine love, that we may ever love You with our whole heart, in word and deed, and never cease praising You.

Give us, O Lord, as much a lasting fear as a lasting love of Your Holy Name, for You, who live and are King for ever and ever, never fail to govern those whom You have solidly established in Your love. Amen.

Litany of Our Lady of Seven Sorrows

Lord, have mercy on us.

Christ, have mercy on us.

Lord, have mercy on us.

Christ, hear us. Christ, graciously hear us.

God, the Father of heaven, Have mercy on us.

God the Son, Redeemer of the world, Have mercy on us.

God the Holy Ghost, Have mercy on us.

Holy Mary, Mother of God, pray for us.

Holy Virgin of virgins, pray for us.

Mother of the Crucified, pray for us.

Sorrowful Mother, pray for us.

Mournful Mother, pray for us.

Sighing Mother, pray for us.

Afflicted Mother, pray for us.

Forsaken Mother, pray for us.

Desolate Mother, pray for us.

Mother most sad, pray for us.

Mother set around with anguish, pray for us.

Mother overwhelmed by grief, pray for us.

Mother transfixed by a sword, pray for us.

Mother crucified in thy heart, pray for us.

Mother bereaved of thy Son, pray for us.

Sighing Dove, pray for us.

Mother of Dolors, pray for us.

Fount of tears, pray for us.

Sea of bitterness, pray for us.

Field of tribulation, pray for us.

Mass of suffering, pray for us.

Mirror of patience, pray for us.

Rock of constancy, pray for us.

Remedy in perplexity, pray for us.

Joy of the afflicted, pray for us.

Ark of the desolate, pray for us.

Refuge of the abandoned, pray for us.

Shield of the oppressed, pray for us.

Conqueror of the incredulous, pray for us.

Solace of the wretched, pray for us.

Medicine of the sick, pray for us.

Help of the faint, pray for us.

Strength of the weak, pray for us.

Protectress of those who fight, pray for us.

Haven of the shipwrecked, pray for us.

Calmer of tempests, pray for us.
Companion of the sorrowful, pray for us.
Retreat of those who groan, pray for us.
Terror of the treacherous, pray for us.
Standard-bearer of the Martyrs, pray for us.
Treasure of the Faithful, pray for us.
Light of Confessors, pray for us.
Pearl of Virgins, pray for us.
Comfort of Widows, pray for us.
Joy of all Saints, pray for us.
Queen of thy Servants, pray for us.
Holy Mary, who alone art unexampled, pray for us.

Pray for us, most Sorrowful Virgin, that we may be
made worthy of the promises of Christ.

Let us pray. O God, in whose Passion, according to the
prophecy of Simeon, a sword of grief pierced through the
most sweet soul of Thy glorious Blessed Virgin Mother
Mary: grant that we, who celebrate the memory of her Seven
Sorrows, may obtain the happy effect of Thy Passion, Who
lives and reigns world without end. Amen.

Act of Reparation to the Immaculate Heart of Mary

O Most Holy Virgin Mother, we listen with grief to the
complaints of your Immaculate Heart surrounded with the
thorns placed therein at every moment by the blasphemies
and ingratitude of ungrateful humanity. We are moved
by the ardent desire of loving you as Our Mother and of
promoting a true devotion to your Immaculate Heart. We
therefore kneel before you to manifest the sorrow we feel

for the grievances that people cause you, and to atone by our prayers and sacrifices for the offenses with which they return your love. Obtain for them and for us the pardon of so many sins. Hasten the conversion of sinners that they may love Jesus and cease to offend the Lord, already so much offended. Turn your eyes of mercy toward us, that we may love God with all our heart on earth and enjoy Him forever in heaven. Amen.

Sacred Scripture for Times of Emergency

Through Sacred Scripture, we can "share in the good things of God that utterly exceed the intelligence of the human mind."[140] But for this to happen, we must hear Sacred Scripture, understand Sacred Scripture, and pray Sacred Scripture within the Holy Tradition of the Church. When we most need his guidance, advice, and support in times of emergency, God will speak to us through Sacred Scripture and Holy Tradition. Having said this, we must be in the right place to hear him, knowing that his Word is the measure of human thinking, not human thinking the measure of his Word:

> For my thoughts are not your thoughts,
> nor are your ways my ways, says the LORD.
> For as the heavens are higher than the earth,
> so are my ways higher than your ways
> and my thoughts than your thoughts. (Is 55:8–9)

The essential thing to realize is that God may give you an answer you will not expect, or at first you may not understand or may not even want to hear. This is why the obedience of faith is so necessary in our response to God's Word:

---

[140]   First Vatican Council, *Dei Filius*, 113.

"By faith, man completely submits his intellect and his will to God. With his whole being man gives his assent to God the revealer. Sacred Scripture calls this human response to God, the author of revelation, 'the obedience of faith' (Rom 1:5; 16:26). To obey (from the Latin ob-audire, to 'hear or listen to') in faith is to submit freely to the word that has been heard, because its truth is guaranteed by God, who is Truth itself. Abraham is the model of such obedience offered us by Sacred Scripture. The Virgin Mary is its most perfect embodiment" (CCC 143–44).

The following passages of Sacred Scripture have been selected to help you hear the living Word of God in any emergency you may face.

God's Directions on How to Face Emergencies

Do not let your hearts be troubled. Believe in God, believe also in me. (Jn 14:1)

Peace I leave with you; my peace I give you. I do not give to you as the world gives. Do not let your hearts be troubled, and do not let them be afraid. (Jn 14:27–28)

On that day, when evening had come, he said to them, "Let us go across to the other side." And leaving the crowd behind, they took him with them in the boat, just as he was. Other boats were with him. A great windstorm arose, and the waves beat into the boat, so that the boat was already being swamped. But he was in the stern, asleep on the cushion; and they woke him up and said to him, "Teacher, do you not care that we are perishing?" He woke up and rebuked the wind, and said to the sea, "Peace! Be still!" Then the wind ceased, and there was a dead calm. He said to them, "Why are you afraid? Have you still no faith?" And they were filled with great awe and said to one another, "Who then is this, that even the wind and the sea obey him?" (Mk 4:35–41)

I hereby command you: Be strong and courageous; do not be frightened or dismayed, for the LORD your God is with you wherever you go. (Jo 1:9)

The LORD will fight for you, and you have only to keep still. (Ex 14:14)

For surely I know the plans I have for you, says the LORD, plans for your welfare and not for harm, to give you a future with hope. Then when you call upon me and come and pray to me, I will hear you. When you search for me, you will find me; if you seek me with all your heart, I will let you find me, says the LORD. (Jer 29:11–14)

Though the Lord may give you the bread of adversity and the water of affliction, yet your Teacher will not hide himself any more, but your eyes shall see your Teacher. And when you turn to the right or when you turn to the left, your ears shall hear a word behind you, saying, "This is the way; walk in it." (Is 30: 20–21)

It is the LORD who goes before you. He will be with you; he will not fail you or forsake you. Do not fear or be dismayed. (Dt 31:8)

Call on me in the day of trouble; I will deliver you, and you shall glorify me. (Ps 50:15)

But now thus says the LORD,
he who created you, O Jacob,
he who formed you, O Israel:
Do not fear, for I have redeemed you;
I have called you by name, you are mine.

When you pass through the waters, I will be with
   you;
and through the rivers, they shall not overwhelm you;
when you walk through fire you shall not be burned,
and the flame shall not consume you. (Is 43:1–2)

Do not fear, for I am with you,
do not be afraid, for I am your God;
I will strengthen you, I will help you,
I will uphold you with my victorious right hand. (Is
   41:10)

Have Faith That Jesus Has Conquered the World

In the world you face persecution. But take courage: I have
conquered the world (Jn 16: 33)

My sheep hear my voice. I know them, and they follow me.
I give them eternal life, and they will never perish. No one
will snatch them out of my hand. What my Father has given
me is greater than all else, and no one can snatch it out of
the Father's hand. The Father and I are one. (Jn 10:27–30)

For whatever is born of God conquers the world! And this is
the victory that conquers the world, our faith. Who is it that
conquers the world but the one who believes that Jesus is the
Son of God? (1 Jn 5:4–5)

Little children, you are from God, and have conquered them; for the one who is in you is greater than the one who is in the world. (1 Jn 4:4)

But they have conquered him by the blood of the Lamb and by the word of their testimony, for they did not cling to life even in the face of death. (Rv 12:11)

Take a Biblical Approach to Emergencies

Blessed be the God and Father of our Lord Jesus Christ! By his great mercy he has given us a new birth into a living hope through the resurrection of Jesus Christ from the dead, and into an inheritance that is imperishable, undefiled, and unfading, kept in heaven for you, who are being protected by the power of God through faith for a salvation ready to be revealed in the last time. In this you rejoice, even if now for a little while you have had to suffer various trials, so that the genuineness of your faith—being more precious than gold that, though perishable, is tested by fire—may be found to result in praise and glory and honor when Jesus Christ is revealed. Although you have not seen him, you love him; and even though you do not see him now, you believe in him and rejoice with an indescribable and glorious joy, for you are receiving the outcome of your faith, the salvation of your souls. (1 Pt 1:3–9)

I consider that the sufferings of this present time are not worth comparing with the glory about to be revealed to us. (Rom 8:18)

We know that all things work together for good for those who love God, who are called according to his purpose. (Rom 8:28)

If God is for us, who is against us? (Rom 8:31)

Who will separate us from the love of Christ? Will hardship, or distress, or persecution, or famine, or nakedness, or peril, or sword? As it is written,

> "For your sake we are being killed all day long;
>   we are accounted as sheep to be slaughtered."

No, in all these things we are more than conquerors through him who loved us. For I am convinced that neither death, nor life, nor angels, nor rulers, nor things present, nor things to come, nor powers, nor height, nor depth, nor anything else in all creation, will be able to separate us from the love of God in Christ Jesus our Lord. (Rom 8:35–39)

Submit yourselves therefore to God. Resist the devil, and he will flee from you. Draw near to God, and he will draw near to you. (Jas 4:7–8)

We have this hope, a sure and steadfast anchor of the soul. (Jas 6:19)

> Trust in the LORD with all your heart,
>   and do not rely on your own insight.
> In all your ways acknowledge him,
>   and he will make straight your paths.
> Do not be wise in your own eyes;
>   fear the LORD, and turn away from evil.

It will be a healing for your flesh
  and a refreshment for your body. (Prv 3:5–8)

My child, do not let these escape from your sight:
  keep sound wisdom and prudence,
and they will be life for your soul
  and adornment for your neck.
Then you will walk on your way securely
  and your foot will not stumble.
If you sit down, you will not be afraid;
  when you lie down, your sleep will be sweet.
Do not be afraid of sudden panic,
  or of the storm that strikes the wicked;
for the LORD will be your confidence
  and will keep your foot from being caught. (Prv
  3:21–26)

The LORD is good to those who wait for him,
  to the soul that seeks him.
It is good that one should wait quietly
  for the salvation of the LORD.
It is good for one to bear
  the yoke in youth,
to sit alone in silence
  when the Lord has imposed it,
to put one's mouth to the dust
  (there may yet be hope),
to give one's cheek to the smiter,
  and be filled with insults. (Lam 3:25–30)

I believe that I shall see the goodness of the LORD
   in the land of the living.
Wait for the LORD;
   be strong, and let your heart take courage;
   wait for the LORD! (Ps 27:13–14)

The LORD is the everlasting God,
   the Creator of the ends of the earth.
He does not faint or grow weary;
   his understanding is unsearchable.
He gives power to the faint,
   and strengthens the powerless.
Even youths will faint and be weary,
   and the young will fall exhausted;
but those who wait for the LORD shall renew their
   strength,
   they shall mount up with wings like eagles,
they shall run and not be weary,
   they shall walk and not faint. (Is 40:28–31)

They are not afraid of evil tidings;
their hearts are firm, secure in the LORD.
Their hearts are steady, they will not be afraid. (Ps
   112:7–8)

My flesh and my heart may fail, but God is the
   strength of my heart and my portion forever. (Ps
   73:26)

Take Refuge in the Lord

But let all who take refuge in you rejoice;
   let them ever sing for joy.
Spread your protection over them,
   so that those who love your name may exult in you.
For you bless the righteous, O Lord;
   you cover them with favor as with a shield. (Ps
   5:11–12)

The Lord is my light and my salvation;
   whom shall I fear?
The Lord is the stronghold of my life;
   of whom shall I be afraid? (Ps 27:1)

For he will hide me in his shelter
   in the day of trouble;
he will conceal me under the cover of his tent;
   he will set me high on a rock. (Ps 27:5)

I love you, O Lord, my strength.
The Lord is my rock, my fortress, and my deliverer,
my God, my rock in whom I take refuge,
my shield, and the horn of my salvation, my stronghold. (Ps 18:1–2)

The Lord is a stronghold for the oppressed,
   a stronghold in times of trouble.
And those who know your name put their trust in
   you,
   for you, O Lord, have not forsaken those who seek
   you. (Ps 9:9–10)

You who live in the shelter of the Most High,
  who abide in the shadow of the Almighty,
will say to the LORD, "My refuge and my fortress;
  my God, in whom I trust."

For he will deliver you from the snare of the fowler
  and from the deadly pestilence;
he will cover you with his pinions,
  and under his wings you will find refuge;
  his faithfulness is a shield and buckler.

You will not fear the terror of the night,
  or the arrow that flies by day,
or the pestilence that stalks in darkness,
  or the destruction that wastes at noonday.

A thousand may fall at your side,
  ten thousand at your right hand,
  but it will not come near you.

You will only look with your eyes
  and see the punishment of the wicked.

Because you have made the LORD your refuge,
  the Most High your dwelling place,
no evil shall befall you,
  no scourge come near your tent.

For he will command his angels concerning you
  to guard you in all your ways.
On their hands they will bear you up,
  so that you will not dash your foot against a stone.

You will tread on the lion and the adder,
   the young lion and the serpent you will trample
   under foot.

Those who love me, I will deliver;
   I will protect those who know my name.

When they call to me, I will answer them;
   I will be with them in trouble,
   I will rescue them and honor them.

With long life I will satisfy them,
   and show them my salvation. (Ps 91)

Trust in the Lord

For where two or three are gathered in my name, I am there
among them. (Mt 18:20)

The LORD, your God, is in your midst,
   a warrior who gives victory;
he will rejoice over you with gladness,
   he will renew you in his love;
he will exult over you with loud singing
as on a day of festival. (Zep 3:17–18)

O Most High, when I am afraid,
   I put my trust in you.
In God, whose word I praise,
   in God I trust; I am not afraid;
   what can flesh do to me? (Ps 56:2–4)

Even though I walk through the darkest valley,
I fear no evil;

for you are with me;
your rod and your staff—
they comfort me. (Ps 23:4)

Ask the Lord for Help

Then Jesus told them a parable about their need to pray always and not to lose heart. He said, "In a certain city there was a judge who neither feared God nor had respect for people. In that city there was a widow who kept coming to him and saying, 'Grant me justice against my opponent.' For a while he refused; but later he said to himself, 'Though I have no fear of God and no respect for anyone, yet because this widow keeps bothering me, I will grant her justice, so that she may not wear me out by continually coming.'" And the Lord said, "Listen to what the unjust judge says. And will not God grant justice to his chosen ones who cry to him day and night? Will he delay long in helping them? I tell you, he will quickly grant justice to them. And yet, when the Son of Man comes, will he find faith on earth?" (Lk 18:1–8)

The Lord is near. Do not worry about anything, but in everything by prayer and supplication with thanksgiving let your requests be made known to God. And the peace of God, which surpasses all understanding, will guard your hearts and your minds in Christ Jesus. (Phil 4:5–7)

He is able for all time to save those who approach God through him, since he always lives to make intercession for them. (Heb 7:25)

The Lord answer you in the day of trouble!
The name of the God of Jacob protect you!
May he send you help from the sanctuary,
and give you support from Zion. (Ps 20:1–2)

Give ear to my words, O Lord;
  give heed to my sighing.
Listen to the sound of my cry,
  my King and my God,
  for to you I pray.
O Lord, in the morning you hear my voice;
  in the morning I plead my case to you, and watch.
  (Ps 5:1–3)

I sought the Lord, and he answered me,
  and delivered me from all my fears.
Look to him, and be radiant;
  so your faces shall never be ashamed.
This poor soul cried, and was heard by the Lord,
  and was saved from every trouble. (Ps 34:4–6)

When the righteous cry for help, the Lord hears,
  and rescues them from all their troubles.
The Lord is near to the brokenhearted,
  and saves the crushed in spirit. (Ps 34:17–18)

Answer me quickly, O Lord;
  my spirit fails.
Do not hide your face from me,
  or I shall be like those who go down to the Pit.
Let me hear of your steadfast love in the morning,
  for in you I put my trust.

Teach me the way I should go,
　for to you I lift up my soul. (Ps 143:7–8)

Words of Hope for Those Who Grieve

Blessed are those who mourn, for they will be comforted. (Mt 5:4)

For God so loved the world that he gave his only Son, so that everyone who believes in him may not perish but may have eternal life. (Jn 3:16)

Jesus said to her, "I am the resurrection and the life. Those who believe in me, even though they die, will live, and everyone who lives and believes in me will never die. Do you believe this?" She said to him, "Yes, Lord, I believe that you are the Messiah, the Son of God, the one coming into the world." (Jn 11:25–27)

When a woman is in labor, she has pain, because her hour has come. But when her child is born, she no longer remembers the anguish because of the joy of having brought a human being into the world. So you have pain now; but I will see you again, and your hearts will rejoice, and no one will take your joy from you. (Jn 16:21–22)

Come to me, all you that are weary and are carrying heavy burdens, and I will give you rest. Take my yoke upon you, and learn from me; for I am gentle and humble in heart, and you will find rest for your souls. For my yoke is easy, and my burden is light. (Mt 11:28–29)

Love bears all things, believes all things, hopes all things, endures all things. (1 Cor 13:7)

But we do not want you to be uninformed, brothers and sisters, about those who have died, so that you may not grieve as others do who have no hope. For since we believe that Jesus died and rose again, even so, through Jesus, God will bring with him those who have died. For this we declare to you by the word of the Lord, that we who are alive, who are left until the coming of the Lord, will by no means precede those who have died. For the Lord himself, with a cry of command, with the archangel's call and with the sound of God's trumpet, will descend from heaven, and the dead in Christ will rise first. Then we who are alive, who are left, will be caught up in the clouds together with them to meet the Lord in the air; and so we will be with the Lord forever. Therefore encourage one another with these words. (1 Thes 4:13–18)

> He will wipe every tear from their eyes.
> Death will be no more;
> mourning and crying and pain will be no more,
> for the first things have passed away. (Rv 21:4)

> He heals the brokenhearted, and binds up their
> wounds. (Ps 147:3)

Prayers for Times of National Emergency

Prayer to Obtain Grace and Mercy in Times of Calamity[141]

Jesus Christ, the King of Glory, comes in peace.
God was made man.
The Word was made flesh.
Christ was born of the Blessed Virgin Mary.
Christ went through the midst of them in peace.
Christ was crucified.
Christ died.
Christ was buried.
Christ rose from the dead.
Christ ascended into heaven.
Christ is victorious.
Christ reigns.
Christ is Lord of all.
May Christ defend us from all evil.

---

[141]   Bishops of England, *The Manual of Prayer* (London: Burns Oates and Washbourne Ltd, 1922), 191–94.

Jesus is with us.

Our Father. Hail Mary. Glory be to the Father.

Eternal Father, by the Blood of Jesus have mercy on us; sign us with the Blood of the Immaculate Lamb Jesus Christ, as You did sign the people of Israel, in order to deliver them from death; and do you, Mary, Mother of Mercy, pray to God, and appease Him for us, and obtain for us the grace we ask.

Glory be to the Father.

Eternal Father, by the Blood of Jesus have mercy on us; save us from the shipwreck of the world, as You did save Noah from the universal deluge: and do you, Mary, Ark of salvation, pray to God and appease Him for us, and obtain for us the grace we ask.

Glory be to the Father.

Eternal Father, by the Blood of Jesus have mercy on us; deliver us from the evils which we have deserved for our sins, as You did deliver Lot from the flames of Sodom: and do you, Mary, our Advocate, pray to God and appease Him for us, and obtain for us the grace we ask.

Glory be to the Father.

Eternal Father, by the Blood of Jesus have mercy on us; comfort us under our present necessities, and troubles, as You did comfort Job, Hannah, and Tobit in their afflictions; and do you, Mary, Comforter of the afflicted, pray to God and appease Him for us, and obtain for us the grace we ask.

Glory be to the Father.

Eternal Father, by the Blood of Jesus have mercy on us; You who does not will the death of a sinner, but rather that he should be converted and live, grant us through Your mercy time for penance, that, filled with contrition and penance for our sins, which are the cause of all our evils, we live in the holy faith, hope, charity, and peace of our Lord Jesus Christ: and do you, Mary, Refuge of sinners, pray to God and appease Him for us, and obtain for us the grace we ask.

Glory be to the Father.

Precious Blood of Jesus, our Love, cry to the Divine Father for mercy, pardon, grace, and peace upon us, [upon N.,] and upon all the world.

Glory be to the Father.

Mary, our Mother and our Hope, pray to God for us, [for N.,] and for all, and obtain for us the grace we ask.

Glory be to the Father.

Eternal Father, we offer You the Blood of Jesus Christ in discharge of all our debt of sin, for the wants of Holy Church and for the conversion of sinners.

Glory be to the Father.

Mary Immaculate, Mother of God, pray to Jesus for us, [for N.,] and for all. Jesu, Mary, mercy!

St. Michael Archangel, St. Joseph, SS. Peter and Paul, protectors of all the faithful in the Church of God, and all Angels and Saints of Paradise, men and women, pray to God and by your intercession obtain grace and mercy for us, [for N.,] and for all. Amen.

Prayers in Times of Calamity[142]

Mercy of our God, encompass us, and deliver us from every plague.

Glory be to the Father.

Eternal Father, sign us with the Blood of the Immaculate Lamb, as You did sign the dwellings of Your people.

Glory be to the Father.

Most Precious Blood of Jesus our Love, cry for mercy for us from Your Divine Father, and deliver us.

Glory be to the Father.

Wounds of Jesus, mouths of love and mercy, speak for us in pity to the Eternal Father; hide us within yourselves and deliver us.

Glory be to the Father.

---

[142]   Ambrose St. John, *The Raccolta of Indulgenced Prayers and Good Works* (Milton Keynes: Hope and Life Press, 2018), 172–73.

Eternal Father, Jesus is ours; ours His Blood, ours His infinite merits; to You we wholly offer ourselves: then, as You love Him, and holdest precious this gift we make to You, You ought to deliver us; for this we hope with full confidence.

Glory be to the Father.

Eternal Father, You do not desire the death of a sinner, but rather that he should be converted and live: in Your mercy grant that we may live before You and be for ever Yours.

Glory be to the Father.

Save us, Christ our Savior, by the virtue of Your Holy Cross; You who saved Peter in the sea, have mercy upon us.

Mary, Mother of mercy, pray for us, and we shall be delivered; Mary, our advocate, speak for us, and we shall be saved.

The Lord justly scourges us for our sins; but do you, Mary, plead for us, for you are our most tender Mother.

Mary, in your Jesus, and in you, we have put our hope; oh, let us never be confounded.

Hail, Holy Queen, Mother of Mercy, our life, our sweetness and our hope! To thee do we cry, poor banished children of Eve. To thee do we send up our sighs, mourning and weeping in this valley of tears! Turn, then, O most gracious Advocate, thine eyes of mercy toward us, and after this, our exile, show unto us the blessed fruit of thy womb, Jesus. O clement, O loving, O sweet Virgin Mary.

V. Pray for us, O holy Mother of God.

R. That we may be made worthy of the promises of Christ. Amen.

In Time of Pestilence[143]

The Litany of Saints (p. 184) is recited, followed by:

Psalm 6

O Lord, do not rebuke me in your anger,
  or discipline me in your wrath.
Be gracious to me, O Lord, for I am languishing;
  O Lord, heal me, for my bones are shaking with
  terror.
My soul also is struck with terror,
  while you, O Lord—how long?

Turn, O Lord, save my life;
  deliver me for the sake of your steadfast love.
For in death there is no remembrance of you;
  in Sheol who can give you praise?

I am weary with my moaning;
  every night I flood my bed with tears;
  I drench my couch with my weeping.
My eyes waste away because of grief;
  they grow weak because of all my foes.

Depart from me, all you workers of evil,
  for the Lord has heard the sound of my weeping.

---

143   Bishops of England, *The Manual of Prayer* (London: Burns Oates and Washbourne Ltd, 1922), 269–78, 241–44.

The Lord has heard my supplication;
   the Lord accepts my prayer.
All my enemies shall be ashamed and struck with
   terror;
   they shall turn back, and in a moment be put to
   shame.

Glory be to the Father.

O Lord, deal not with us according to our sins
   Neither repay us according to our iniquities
Help us, O God our Savior.
   And for the glory of Your Name, O Lord, deliver us.
O Lord, remember not our former iniquities.
   *Let Your mercies speedily preserve us, for we are
   becoming exceedingly poor.*
Pray for us, O holy Sebastian.
   *That we may be made worthy of the promises of
   Christ.*
O Lord, hear my prayer.
   And let my cry come to You.

Let us pray.

Hear us, O God of our salvation, and through the intercession of the blessed and glorious Mother of God, Mary, ever a Virgin, and of Blessed Sebastian the Martyr, deliver Your people from the terrors of Divine anger and make them secure by the bountifulness of Your mercy.

Be appeased, O Lord, by our humble prayers and heal all our sickness of body and soul, so that having received Your forgiveness we may rejoice in Your Blessing.

Grant us, we beseech You, O Lord, a favourable answer to our devout prayers and turn away from us the scourge of pestilence: so that men may confess in their hearts that these punishments come from Your wrath and cease by Your mercy. Through our Lord Jesus Christ, who lives and reigns with You, in the Unity of the Holy Spirit, God, World without end. Amen.

In Times of Storm and Tempest[144]

The Litany of Saints (p. 184) is recited, followed by:

Psalm 147: 12–20

Praise the Lord, O Jerusalem!
Praise your God, O Zion!
For he strengthens the bars of your gates;
he blesses your children within you.
He grants peace within your borders;
he fills you with the finest of wheat.
He sends out his command to the earth;
his word runs swiftly.
He gives snow like wool;
he scatters frost like ashes.
He hurls down hail like crumbs—
who can stand before his cold?

---

[144] Ibid., 245–47.

He sends out his word, and melts them;
he makes his wind blow, and the waters flow.
He declares his word to Jacob,
his statutes and ordinances to Israel.
He has not dealt thus with any other nation;
they do not know his ordinances.
Praise the Lord!

Glory be to the Father, etc.

Our help is in the name of the Lord.
Who has made Heaven and earth.
Show us, O Lord, Your mercy.
And give us Your Salvation.
Help us, O God our Savior.
And for the glory of Your Name, O Lord, deliver us.
Let not the enemy have any advantage over us.
Nor the son of iniquity have power to hurt us.
Let Your mercy, O Lord, be upon us.
Even as we have trusted in You.
Save Your people, O Lord.
And bless their inheritance.
Do not deprive of good things those that walk in
innocence.
O Lord of hosts, blessed is the man that trusts in You.
O Lord, hear my prayer.
And let my cry come to You.

Let us pray.

O God, who are offended by sin and are pacified by penance, mercifully regard the prayers of Your people making supplication to You, and turn away the scourge of Your anger which we deserve for our sins.

We beseech You, O Lord, that the spirits of wickedness may be driven away from Your house and that storms may cease to harass us.

O Lord Jesus, you did rebuke the winds and the sea, and there came a great calm: graciously hear the prayers of Your household and grant that in virtue of this sign of the holy cross we may be spared the havoc wrought by storm and tempest.

Almighty and Everlasting God, who heals by chastening, and keeps by forgiving, grant that we who humbly pray to You, may rejoice in the peace and consolation which we desire and ever enjoy the gift of Your mercy. Through our Lord Jesus Christ, who lives and reigns with You in the unity of the Holy Spirit, God, World without end. Amen.

In Time of War[145]

The Litany of Saints (p. 184) is recited, followed by:

Psalm 46

God is our refuge and strength,
a very present help in trouble.
Therefore we will not fear, though the earth should
   change,
though the mountains shake in the heart of the sea;

---

[145]   Ibid., 248–50.

though its waters roar and foam,
though the mountains tremble with its tumult.

There is a river whose streams make glad the city of
  God,
the holy habitation of the Most High.
God is in the midst of the city; it shall not be moved;
God will help it when the morning dawns.
The nations are in an uproar, the kingdoms totter;
he utters his voice, the earth melts.
The Lord of hosts is with us;
the God of Jacob is our refuge.

Come, behold the works of the Lord;
see what desolations he has brought on the earth.
He makes wars cease to the end of the earth;
he breaks the bow, and shatters the spear;
he burns the shields with fire.
"Be still, and know that I am God!
I am exalted among the nations,
I am exalted in the earth."
The Lord of hosts is with us;
the God of Jacob is our refuge.

Glory be to the Father, etc.

Arise, O Lord, and help us.
And deliver us for Your name's sake.
Save Your people, O Lord.
That hope in You, O my God.
Let peace be in Your Strength.
And abundance in Your Towers.

Be to us, O Lord, a tower of strength.
Before the face of the enemy.
He shall break the bow and snap the weapons in two.
Send us help, O Lord, from Your Holy place.
And defend us out of Zion.
O Lord, hear my prayer.
And let my cry come to You.

Let us pray.

O God, who brings wars to nothing and shields by Your power all those that hope in You, overthrowing those who assail them: help Your servants who implore Your mercy; so that the fierce might of their enemies may be brought low and that we may never cease from praising and thanking You.

O God, from whom are holy desires, right counsels and just works: give to Your servants that peace which the world cannot give; that our hearts may be disposed to obey Your commandments, and, the fear of enemies being removed, our times by Your protection may be tranquil.

We beseech You, O Lord, to crush the pride of our enemies and to humble their insolence by the might of Your Hand. Through our Lord Jesus Christ, Your Son, who lives and reigns with You in the unity of the Holy Spirit, God, world without end. Amen.

The Greater Litanies

For deliverance from all kinds of evil

According to Abbot Gueranger, Pope St. Gregory the Great prescribed praying *The Greater Litanies* in solemn procession for times of public calamity, such as the one famously held to end the plague in AD 591.[146]

The Litany of Saints (p. 184) is recited, followed by:

Psalm 69

O God, make haste to my rescue, Lord, come to my
aid!
Let there be shame and confusion, on those who
seek my life.
O let them turn back in confusion, who delight in
my harm,
let them retreat, covered with shame, who jeer at
my lot.

Let there be rejoicing and gladness for all who seek
You.
Let them say forever: "God is great," who love Your
saving help.
As for me, wretched and poor, come to me, O God.
You are my rescuer, my help, O Lord, do not delay.

Glory be to the Father, and to the Son, and to the
Holy Spirit.

---

146 "The Greater Litanies," https://www.salvemariaregina.info/Salve-MariaRegina/SMR-156/Greater%20Litanies.htm.

As it was in the beginning, is now and ever shall be.
World without end. Amen.

Save your servants.
Who hope in You, O my God.
Be for us, O Lord, a tower of strength.
From the face of the enemy.
Let not the enemy prevail against us.
Nor the son of wickedness have power to hurt us.
O Lord, deal not with us according to our sins.
Neither requite us according to our iniquities.
Let us pray for our Sovereign Pontiff N.
The Lord preserve him, and give him life, and make him
   blessed upon the earth, and deliver him not up to the
   will of his enemies.
Let us pray for our benefactors.
O Lord, for Your name's sake, reward with eternal life
   all those who do us good. Amen.
Let us pray for the faithful departed.
Eternal rest give unto them, O Lord, and let perpetual
   light shine upon them.
May they rest in peace. *Amen.*
For our absent brothers and sisters.
Save Your servants, who hope in You, O my God.
Send them help, O Lord, from the holy place.
And from Sion protect them.
O Lord, hear my prayer.
And let my cry come unto you.
The Lord be with you.
And with your spirit.

Let us pray.

O God, Whose property is always to have mercy and to spare, receive our humble petition: that we, and all Your servants who are bound by the chain of sin, may by the compassion of Your goodness mercifully be absolved.

Graciously hear, we beseech You, O Lord, the prayers of Your suppliants, and forgive the sins of those that confess to You: that, in Your bounty, You may grant us pardon and peace.

In Your clemency, O Lord, show Your unspeakable mercy to us: that You may both loose us from all our sins, and deliver us from the punishments which we deserve for them.

O God, Who by sin are offended, and by penance pacified, mercifully regard the prayers of Your people making supplication to You, and turn away the scourges which we deserve for our sins.

Almighty, everlasting God, have mercy upon Your servant N., our Sovereign Pontiff, and direct him according to Your clemency into the way of everlasting salvation, that by Your grace he may both desire those things that are pleasing to You, and perform them with all his strength.

O God, from Whom are all holy desires, right counsels, and just works, give unto Your servants that peace which the world cannot give; that both our hearts—given over to Your commands—and our times—the fear of our foes removed—may by Your protection be peaceful.

Inflame, O Lord, our hearts with the fire of the Holy Spirit: that we may serve You with a chaste body and please You with a clean heart.

O God, the Creator and Redeemer of all the faithful, grant to the souls of Your servants departed the remission of all their sins: that through pious supplications they may obtain that pardon which they have always desired.

Go before, we beseech You, O Lord, our actions by Your inspirations, and further them by Your assistance; that every word and work of ours may begin always from You, and by You be likewise ended.

Almighty, everlasting God, Who has dominion over the living and the dead, and are merciful to all, of whom You foreknow that they will be Yours by faith and good works: we humbly beseech You, that they for whom we intend to pour forth our prayers, whether this present world still detain them in the flesh, or the world to come has already received them out of their bodies, may, through the intercession of all Your saints, by the clemency of Your goodness, obtain the remission of all their sins.

Through our Lord Jesus Christ Your Son, who lives and reigns with You in the unity of the Holy Spirit, one God, for ever and ever. *Amen.*

The Lord be with you. *And with your spirit.*

May the almighty and merciful Lord graciously hear us. *Amen.*

And may the souls of the faithful departed, through the mercy of God, rest in peace. *Amen.*

The Litany of the Saints

Lord, have mercy on us. *Lord, have mercy on us.*
Christ, have mercy on us. *Christ, have mercy on us.*
Lord, have mercy on us. *Lord, have mercy on us.*
Christ, hear us. *Christ, graciously hear us.*

God the Father of heaven, *have mercy on us.*
God the Son,
Redeemer of the world,
God the Holy Spirit,
Holy Trinity,
One God,

Holy Mary, *pray for us.*
Holy Mother of God,
Holy Virgin of virgins,
Saint Michael,
Saint Gabriel,
Saint Raphael,
All you holy Angels and Archangels,
All you holy orders of blessed spirits,
Saint John the Baptist,
Saint Joseph,
All you holy Patriarchs and Prophets,
Saint Peter,
Saint Paul,
Saint Andrew,
Saint James,

Saint John,

Saint Thomas,

Saint James,

Saint Philip,

Saint Bartholomew,

Saint Matthew,

Saint Simon,

Saint Thaddeus,

Saint Matthias,

Saint Barnabas,

Saint Luke,

Saint Mark,

All you holy Apostles and Evangelists,

All you holy disciples of our Lord, *pray for us*

All you holy Innocents,

Saint Stephen,

Saint Lawrence,

Saint Vincent,

Saints Fabian and Sebastian,

Saints John and Paul,

Saints Cosmas and Damian,

Saints Gervase and Protase,

All you holy Martyrs,

Saint Sylvester,

Saint Gregory,

Saint Ambrose,

Saint Augustine,

Saint Jerome,

Saint Martin,

Saint Nicholas,

All you holy Bishops and Confessors,
All you holy Doctors,
Saint Anthony,
Saint Benedict,
Saint Bernard,
Saint Dominic,
Saint Francis,
All you holy Priests and Levites,
All you holy Monks and Hermits,
Saint Mary Magdalen,
Saint Agatha,
Saint Lucy,
Saint Agnes,
Saint Cecily,
Saint Catherine,
Saint Anastasia,
All you holy Virgins and Widows,

All you holy men and women, Saints of God, *make intercession for us.*

Be merciful, *spare us O Lord.*
Be merciful, *graciously hear us O Lord.*
From all evil, *deliver us, O Lord.*
From all sin,
From Your wrath,

(Petition added in Time of Pestilence)
From pestilence and famine, *deliver us, O Lord.*
  (Repeat twice)

(Petition added in *Time of Storm and Tempest*)
From storms and tempest, *deliver us, O Lord. (Repeat twice)*

From the scourge of earthquake, *deliver us, O Lord.*
From plague, famine and war,
From sudden and unprovided death,
From the snares of the devil,
From anger, hatred, and all ill-will,
From the spirit of fornication,
From lightening and tempest,
From everlasting death,
Through the mystery of Your holy Incarnation,
Through Your coming,
Through Your nativity,
Through Your baptism and holy fasting,
Through Your Cross and Passion,
Through Your death and burial,
Through Your holy Resurrection,
Through Your admirable Ascension,
Through the coming of the Holy Spirit the Paraclete,
In day of judgement,
We sinners, *we beseech You, hear us.*
That You would deliver us from the scourge of pestilence,
That You would spare us,
That You would pardon us,
That You would bring us to true penance,
That You would govern and preserve Your holy Church,

That You would preserve our Pope and all orders of
the Church in holy religion,

That You would humble the enemies of the Church,

That You would grant peace and unity to all Christian people,

That You would confirm and preserve us in Your holy
service,

That You would lift up our minds to heavenly desires,

That You would render eternal blessings to all our
benefactors,

That You would deliver our souls, and the souls of
our brethren, relations and benefactors, from eternal damnation,

That You would give and preserve the fruit of the
earth,

That You would give eternal rest to all the faithful
departed,

That You would graciously hear us,

Son of God,

Lamb of God, Who take away the sins of the world,
Spare us, O Lord.

Lamb of God, Who take away the sins of the world,
Graciously hear us, O Lord.

Lamb of God, Who take away the sins of the world,
Have mercy on us.

Christ, hear us. *Christ, graciously hear us.*

Lord, have mercy on us. *Christ, have mercy on us.*

Lord, have mercy on us.

A Brief Guide to Indulgences

The Baltimore Catechism on Indulgences

Q. 839. What is an Indulgence?

A. An Indulgence is the remission in whole or in part of the temporal punishment due to sin.

Q. 840. What does the word "indulgence" mean?

A. The word indulgence means a favor or concession. An indulgence obtains by a very slight penance the remission of penalties that would otherwise be severe.

Q. 841. Is an Indulgence a pardon of sin, or a license to commit sin?

A. An Indulgence is not a pardon of sin, nor a license to commit sin, and one who is in a state of mortal sin cannot gain an Indulgence.

Q. 843. How many kinds of Indulgences are there?

A. There are two kinds of Indulgences—Plenary and Partial.

Q. 844. What is Plenary Indulgence?

A. A Plenary Indulgence is the full remission of the temporal punishment due to sin.

Q. 845. Is it easy to gain a Plenary Indulgence?

A. It is not easy to gain a Plenary Indulgence, as we may understand from its great privilege. To gain a Plenary Indulgence, we must hate sin, be heartily sorry for even our venial sins, and have no desire for even the slightest sin. Though we may not gain entirely each Plenary Indulgence we seek, we always gain a part of each; that is, a partial indulgence, greater or less in proportion to our good dispositions.

Q. 847. What is a Partial Indulgence?

A Partial Indulgence is the remission of part of the temporal punishment due to sin.

Q. 853. How does the Church by means of Indulgences remit the temporal punishment due to sin?

A. The Church, by means of Indulgences, remits the temporal punishment due to sin by applying to us the merits of Jesus Christ, and the superabundant satisfactions of the Blessed Virgin Mary and of the saints; which merits and satisfactions are its spiritual treasury.

A Word on Indulgences by St. John Bosco[147]

You already know, my dear boys, from your catechism what is meant by indulgences. You know that there are Partial Indulgences, which remit only a portion of the temporal punishment due to sin, and Plenary Indulgences, which remit the whole of it, so that, were a person to die immediately after gaining a plenary indulgence, he would go straight to heaven. With what earnestness therefore should not the devout Catholic endeavor to gain as many indulgences as he can both on his own behalf and in suffrage for the souls departed! To gain indulgences, however, certain conditions are required, which shall be briefly explained here.

1. We must be in the grace of God; for He will certainly not remit the punishment, so long as the guilt of sin remains. It is necessary, therefore, to be in the state of grace, which we have either preserved or else regained by means of the sacrament of penance. A single mortal sin weighing upon our conscience is enough to prevent us from gaining the smallest indulgence. Moreover, the existence of a secret attachment to even one venial sin renders us incapable of gaining the full benefit of a plenary indulgence. For partial indulgences, however, it is sufficient to make an act of true contrition, and to have the firm resolve to go to confession.

2. We must also have the intention, at least habitual, of gaining the indulgence; wherefore it is an excellent practice to renew each morning our intention of gaining all the indulgences we can during the course of the day.

---

147 St. John Bosco, *The Companion of Youth* (London: The Salesian Press, 1954), 311–13.

3. Finally, we must perform the good works attached to the indulgence, observing the time and the manner prescribed. As regards the time, if this is not fixed by the Church, we may choose any moment of the natural day, from midnight to midnight. As regards the manner, the prayers may be said alternately with other persons, as is often done in reciting the rosary; they may be said in any language, provided the version is correct; and there is no need to kneel down, unless this condition is explicitly indicated.

Furthermore, for plenary indulgences, Confession and Communion are usually required, as well as a visit to a church or public oratory, and prayers for the intention of the Sovereign Pontiff. When confession is imposed as a condition, it is required even of those who are not in the state of mortal sin; they are not obliged, however, to make their confession on the day on which they are to gain the indulgence, but they may go to confession at any time during the week which precedes or which follows that day. Moreover, those who make it a practice to go to confession about once a fortnight unless prevented from doing so by some grave difficulty, or who receive Holy Communion daily in the state of grace and with a right intention, can gain all indulgences except those of ordinary or extraordinary jubilees, even without actual confession, which would otherwise be necessary. Communion is considered to be daily even if omitted once or twice during the week. One and the same Communion will serve to gain several plenary indulgences on the same day. Where no particular church is specified, the visit may be made in any Church or public Oratory. Note, however, that when it is a case of gaining several plenary indulgences, one distinct visit must be made for each indulgence, so that, after making one visit, it is necessary to leave the church and go in again for the next. The visit may be made before or after fulfilling the other good works, provided it is finished within the prescribed time.

Any particular plenary indulgence can only be gained once in the day, except what is known as the *toties quoties*, which can be gained as often as one wishes. The plenary indulgence which can be gained on All Souls Day is an example of this. No attention should be paid to any leaflets of prayers with indulgences, unless it carries definite statement of ecclesiastical approval. And finally, do not have anything whatever to do with the so-called "chain prayers."

LAUS DEO ET MARIÆ

Emergency Baptism

The Canon Law of the Church makes it clear that an infant or adult in danger of death can be lawfully baptized, due to the necessity of baptism for supernatural life and for salvation.

Can. 849. Baptism, the gateway to the sacraments is necessary for salvation by actual reception or at least by desire. It is validly conferred only by a washing of true water with the proper form of words. Through baptism men and women are freed from sin, are reborn as children of God, and, configured to Christ by an indelible character, and are incorporated into the Church.

Any member of the faithful must administer the sacrament of baptism if an infant, or an adult if they request it, is in imminent danger of death and no priest or deacon is available.

All lay persons, since they belong to the priestly people, and especially parents and, by reason of their work, catechists, obstetricians, women who are employed as family or social workers or as nurses of the sick, as well as physicians and surgeons, should know the proper method of baptizing in cases of necessity (Rite of Baptism 16).

All lay people should know the proper method of baptizing in cases of necessity.

All lay persons, since they belong to the priestly people, and especially parents and, by reason of their work, catechists, obstetricians, . . . nurses of the sick, as well as physicians and surgeons, should know the proper method of baptizing in cases of necessity (Rite of Baptism 17).

It is desirable, though not essential, that the emergency baptism is conferred in the presence of one or two witnesses

How to Administer an Emergency Baptism

You must pour water three times over the person's head while saying these words:

> **N., I baptize you in the name of the Father,** *while pouring water on the person's head the first time.*
> **and of the Son,** *while pouring water on the person's head the second time.*
> **and of the Holy Spirit,** *while pouring water on the person's head the third time.*

Details of the baptism must be given to the parish priest of the place in which the baptism was conferred.

Can. 877 §1. The pastor of the place where the baptism is celebrated must carefully and without any delay record in the baptismal register the names of the baptized, with mention made of the minister, parents, sponsors, witnesses, if any, the place and date of the conferral of the baptism, and the date and place of birth.

About the Author

Deacon Nick Donnelly is a permanent deacon of the Diocese of Lancaster in England. He has served as a diocesan advisor on pastoral renewal, a diocesan consultant in adult formation and has written catechetical programs for various dioceses. He was a co-founder of the School of the Annunciation, England. He is the author of over seventeen books for the Catholic Truth Society, has worked for EWTN GB, and has written for Church Militant, National Catholic Register, LifeSite News, Catholic Voice Ireland and the traditional blog Rorate Caeli. He runs the popular twitter site, @protectthefaith.

Printed in Great Britain
by Amazon